HITLER'S SHADOW

Nazi War Criminals, U.S. Intelligence, and the Cold War

Richard Breitman and Norman J.W. Goda

Published by the National Archives

CONTENTS

PREFACE

In 1998 Congress passed the Nazi War Crimes Disclosure Act [P.L. 105-246] as part of a series of efforts to identify, declassify, and release federal records on the perpetration of Nazi war crimes and on Allied efforts to locate and punish war criminals. Under the direction of the National Archives the Interagency Working Group [IWG] opened to research over 8 million of pages of records - including recent 21st century documentation. Of particular importance to this volume are many declassified intelligence records from the Central Intelligence Agency and the Army Intelligence Command, which were not fully processed and available at the time that the IWG issued its Final Report in 2007.

As a consequence, Congress [in HR 110-920] charged the National Archives in 2009 to prepare an additional historical volume as a companion piece to its 2005 volume *U. S. Intelligence and the Nazis.* Professors Richard Breitman and Norman J. W. Goda note in *Hitler's Shadow* that these CIA & Army records produced new "evidence of war crimes and about wartime activities of war criminals; postwar documents on the search for war criminals; documents about the escape of war criminals; documents about the Allied protection or use of war criminals; and documents about the postwar activities of war criminals".

This volume of essays points to the significant impact that flowed from Congress and the Executive Branch agencies in adopting a broader and fuller release of previously security classified war crimes documentation. Details about records processed by the IWG and released by the National Archives are more fully described on our website *iwg@nara.gov.*

William Cunliffe, Office of Records Services,
National Archives and Records Administration

INTRODUCTION

At the end of World War II, Allied armies recovered a large portion of the written or filmed evidence of the Holocaust and other forms of Nazi persecution. Allied prosecutors used newly found records in numerous war crimes trials. Governments released many related documents regarding war criminals during the second half of the 20th century. A small segment of American-held documents from Nazi Germany or about Nazi officials and Nazi collaborators, however, remained classified into the 21st century because of government restrictions on the release of intelligence-related records.

Approximately 8 million pages of documents declassified in the United States under the 1998 Nazi War Crimes Disclosure Act added significantly to our knowledge of wartime Nazi crimes and the postwar fate of suspected war criminals. A 2004 U.S. Government report by a team of independent historians working with the government's Nazi War Criminal Records Interagency Working Group (IWG), entitled *U.S. Intelligence and the Nazis,* highlighted some of the new information; it appeared with revisions as a 2005 book.[1] Our 2010 report serves as an addendum to *U.S. Intelligence and the Nazis;* it draws upon additional documents declassified since then.

The latest CIA and Army files have: evidence of war crimes and about the wartime activities of war criminals; postwar documents on the search for or prosecution of war criminals; documents about the escape of war criminals; documents about the Allied protection or use of Nazi war criminals; and documents about the postwar political activities of war criminals. None of the declassified documents conveys a complete story in itself; to make sense of this evidence, we have also drawn on older documents and published works.

The Timing of Declassification

Why did the most recent declassifications take so long? In 2005–07 the Central Intelligence Agency adopted a more liberal interpretation of the 1998 Nazi War Crimes Disclosure Act. As a result, CIA declassified and turned over to the National Archives and Records Administration (NARA) additional documents from pre-existing files as well as entirely new CIA files, totaling more than 1,100 files in all. Taken together, there were several thousand pages of new CIA records that no one outside the CIA had seen previously.

A much larger collection came from the Army. In the early postwar years, the Army had the largest U.S. intelligence and counterintelligence organizations in Europe; it also led the search for Nazi war criminals. In 1946 Army intelligence (G-2) and the Army Counterintelligence Corps (CIC) had little competition— the CIA was not established until a year later. Even afterwards, the Army remained a critical factor in intelligence work in central Europe.

Years ago the Army facility at Fort Meade, Maryland, turned over to NARA its classified Intelligence and Security Command Records for Europe from the period (approximately) 1945–63. Mostly counterintelligence records from the Army's Investigative Records Repository (IRR), this collection promised to be a rich source of information about whether the United States maintained an interest in war crimes and Nazi war criminals.

After preserving these records on microfilm, and then on a now obsolete system of optical disks, the Army destroyed many of the paper documents. But the microfilm deteriorated, and NARA could not read or recover about half of the files on the optical disks, let alone declassify and make them available. NARA needed additional resources and technology to solve the technological problems and transfer the IRR files to a special computer server. Declassification of these IRR files only began in 2009, after the IWG had gone out of existence.

This new Army IRR collection comprises 1.3 million files and many millions of pages. It will be years before all of these Army files are available for researchers.

For this report we have drawn selectively upon hundreds of these IRR files, amounting to many thousands of pages, which have been declassified and are already available at NARA.

Intelligence Organizations and War Crimes

American intelligence and counterintelligence organizations each had its own raison d'être, its own institutional interests, and its own priorities. Unfortunately, intelligence officials generally did not record their general policies and attitudes toward war crimes and war criminals, so that we hunted for evidence in their handling of individual cases. Despite variations, these specific cases do show a pattern: the issue of capturing and punishing war criminals became less important over time. During the last months of the war and shortly after it, capturing enemies, collecting evidence about them, and punishing them seemed quite consistent. Undoubtedly, the onset of the Cold War gave American intelligence organizations new functions, new priorities, and new foes. Settling scores with Germans or German collaborators seemed less pressing; in some cases, it even appeared counterproductive.

In the months after the war in Europe ended Allied forces struggled to comprehend the welter of Nazi organizations. Allied intelligence agencies initially scrutinized their German intelligence counterparts for signs of participation in underground organizations, resistance, or sabotage. Assessing threats to the Allied occupation of Germany, they thought first of Nazi fanatics and German intelligence officials. Nazi officials in the concentration camps had obviously committed terrible crimes, but the evidence about the Gestapo was not as striking. The Allies started by trying to find out who had been responsible for what.

NOTES

1 Richard Breitman, Norman J.W. Goda, Timothy Naftali, and Robert Wolfe, *U.S. Intelligence and the Nazis* (New York: Cambridge University Press, 2005).

Gertrude (Traudl) Junge, one of Hitler's personal secretaries, stayed in the Reichschancellery bunker to take Hitler's last will and testament before his suicide. Junge describes the perils in working her way through the Russian lines surrounding Berlin. She relates meeting Hitler's chauffeur Kemka and of the deaths of Martin Bormann, Stumpfegger, and Naumann, when their armored car was blown up.
RG 319, Records of the Army Staff.

CHAPTER ONE

New Information on Major Nazi Figures

Newly released Army records yield bits of intriguing information collected by the Army Counterintelligence Corps (CIC) after the war about some leading officials of the Nazi regime. The new information tends to confirm rather than change what historians have known about leading Nazi functionaries and their postwar fates. At the same time, it provides sharper focus than before.

New Interrogations of Hitler's Personal Secretary

Gertraud (Traudl) Junge, Adolf Hitler's secretary starting in January 1943, took the dictation for Hitler's final testaments on April 29, 1945, the night before Hitler committed suicide. On May 2, 1945, she fled Hitler's bunker in Berlin with a small group, trying to move through Soviet lines to safety. The Soviets captured her on June 3. They imprisoned and interrogated her in their sector of Berlin. She left Berlin and went to Munich in April 1946.

Junge's recollections are an important source for Hitler's final days in the bunker. Soviet intelligence took great pains to confirm Hitler's death amidst persistent rumors that he was still alive, as did Allied investigators.[1] (Soviet interrogations of Junge have not yet surfaced.) On her return to Munich she gave many statements, most of which are well known to scholars. They include a series of interviews in Munich by U.S. Judge Michael Musmanno in February and March 1948 when Musmanno was investigating the circumstances of Hitler's death.[2] She also wrote a personal memoir in 1947, made available to scholars in Munich's Institute for Contemporary History and published in 2002.[3] She gave testimony to German authorities in 1954 as well as numerous interviews to journalists in the years after the war, most famously in a 2002 German documentary film titled *Im toten Winkel* (Blind Spot). She died the same year at age 81.

On June 9, 1946, the CIC Field Office in Starnberg arrested Junge in Munich, and CIC agents interrogated her on June 13 and June 18. On August 30, CIC agents interviewed her a third time at the request of British intelligence, this time with 15 specific British questions. These summer 1946 interrogations are not cited in scholarly works on Hitler's final days. Possibly released here for the first time, they contain occasional detail and nuance that the other statements do not, because they were Junge's first statements on returning to the West.

In the first session Junge recalled Hitler's personal habits, confirming, albeit in new language, what is well known. She recounted Hitler's withdrawn behavior after the German military defeat at Stalingrad in early 1943, his insistence that Germany's miracle weapons would end the Allied bombing of German cities, and his belief that Providence protected him from the July 20, 1944, assassination attempt. Junge remembered Hitler saying that if Claus von Stauffenberg, the leader of the conspiracy, would have shot Hitler face to face instead of using a bomb, then von Stauffenberg would at least be worthy of respect. This interrogation also confirmed the death of Nazi Party Secretary Martin Bormann by Soviet shelling in Berlin. Hitler's chauffeur Erich Kempka witnessed Bormann's death and told Junge about it shortly afterwards. In July 1946 Kempka gave the same story to the International Military Tribunal.[4] At the time many people thought that Bormann escaped and fled to South America. His remains were not discovered until 1999.[5]

The second interrogation provides new detail on Junge's attempted escape from Berlin after Hitler's death, her arrest by the Soviets on June 3, 1945, and her repeated interrogations by the Soviets concerning Hitler's suicide. The Soviets were also interested in any connections Junge might have to existing Nazi networks; they hoped to use her to uncover them. In September 1945, an unnamed Soviet official offered Junge his personal protection including an apartment, food, and money. In return, Junge was to cooperate with Soviet forces and not to tell anyone of her former or present job. She was not to leave the Soviet sector; but after she contracted diphtheria, she was allowed admission to the hospital in the British sector. On leaving the hospital, she said, "the Russians did not take any more interest in my person." She left for Munich and arrived on April 20, 1946.[6]

Her third interrogation benefited from the direct questions from the British. Junge noted that Hitler hoped to delay his suicide until receiving confirmation that the couriers carrying copies of his last political testament had reached their recipients, namely Grand Admiral Karl Dönitz, whom Hitler appointed head of state, and Field Marshal Ferdinand Schörner, whom he appointed army commander-in-chief. With the ring closing around his Berlin bunker, Hitler would not allow the Soviets to take him alive. But he knew Dönitz, whose headquarters was near the Danish border, and Schörner, whose headquarters was in Czechoslovakia, would fight until the last cartridge and hang as many deserters as need be. "Hitler was uneasy," recalled Junge, "and walked from one room to another. He said that he would wait until the couriers had arrived to their destinations with the testaments and then he would commit suicide."[7] The couriers were not able to leave the Berlin area.

The British were also very interested in Hitler's Gestapo chief, Heinrich Müller, who would have offered a treasure trove of counterintelligence information on the Soviets. Allied counterintelligence officers failed to locate him after the war. Some leads placed him in Berlin at war's end and others suggested that he had fled south. The absence of an arrest or even a corpse led to later conspiracy theories that Müller worked for either Allied or Soviet intelligence. The bulk of the evidence, pieced together over the next quarter century, indicates that Müller was killed in Berlin during the war's final days.[8]

Junge was asked directly: "On what occasions did you see Mueller in the Bunker? What do you know of his movements or activities during the last days?" Junge did not know Müller personally. She noted that she saw him for the first time on April 22, 1945. "Mueller remained in the shelter until Hitler's death," she said. "I … observed him talking some times (sic) with Hitler…." Junge continued, "I do not know any details about his activities. He had taken over the functions of [Reich Security Main Office Chief Ernst] Kaltenbrunner…."[9]

At the time of Hitler's suicide, Kaltenbrunner was in Salzburg. He had searched for a negotiated peace through various channels while also hoping that an Alpine front could keep Germany from defeat.[10] What Hitler knew of these efforts in late April 1945 is not clear. But in his political testament he expelled Heinrich Himmler from the Nazi Party owing to Himmler's contacts with the Allies. Hitler promoted Karl Hanke, the fanatical Gauleiter of Lower Silesia who defended Breslau at the cost of some 40,000 civilian lives, to Himmler's office of Reichsführer-SS. Kaltenbrunner was logically the next in line for Himmler's job. Junge's statement suggests that Hitler lost trust in Kaltenbrunner, that Müller remained loyal to the end, and that Hitler trusted in his loyalty.

New Documents: Arthur Greiser's Briefcases

Arthur Greiser, Nazi Gauleiter of the German-annexed portion of western Poland called the Warthegau, was a major war criminal by any standard or definition. Once conquered by the Germans in 1939, the Warthegau region was to be emptied of Jews and Poles and settled with ethnic Germans. The Warthegau also included the Lodz ghetto—the second largest in occupied Poland—and the extermination facility at Chelmno where Jews were first gassed to death. Thus, Greiser helped to implement Nazi policies that killed tens of thousands of expellees as well as more than 150,000 mostly Jews in Chelmo itself.[11] The U.S. Army captured Greiser in Salzburg on May 17, 1945, and extradited him to Poland. Using documents and witness testimony, a Supreme National Tribunal in Warsaw tried and convicted him in June and July 1946. He was hanged in mid-July.[12]

When Greiser fled west in 1945, he carried with him two briefcases filled with documents, mostly dealing with his activities during the 1930s and his personal affairs. Either he left behind or destroyed documents that connected him with policies of mass murder in the Warthegau, or what he kept of those documents went to Polish authorities. Still, the U.S. Army retained more than 2,000 pages of Greiser's documents in the Investigative Records Repository that only now are declassified.[13]

Some of the most interesting documents involve Greiser's activities, from November 1934 and afterwards, as president of the Senate of the international free city of Danzig. This post made Greiser chief executive of a German-dominated municipal government frequently in conflict with the Polish state that surrounded it. How far to push these conflicts provoked discussion and debate among the highest Nazi authorities in Berlin.

Greiser wrote memoranda of his discussions with Hitler, Hermann Göring, Foreign Minister Konstantin von Neurath, his successor Joachim von Ribbentrop, and others. The documents show conflicting views in Berlin about how best to deal with the Poles and the League of Nations. Hitler and the Nazi Party Gauleiter of Danzig, Albert Forster, often wanted confrontation; Göring and Greiser, a more moderate course. Political disagreements help to explain the bitter personal rivalry between Greiser and Forster. Greiser's documents do not challenge the reigning historical consensus about these matters, but they do fill in the narrative. They also underscore—as historians have long argued—that Danzig's foreign policy was made in Berlin.[14]

In 1939 Hitler used conflicts over Danzig as the pretext for Germany to invade Poland. After the war, the Allies decided to charge high Nazi authorities with crimes against peace; the International Military Tribunal at Nuremberg made crimes against peace the central count of four charges against high Nazi officials and organizations; the others were war crimes, crimes against humanity, and conspiracy. The Greiser file contains new evidence about the background to German aggression against Poland and thus about war crimes.

The Search for Adolf Eichmann: New Materials

Today, the world knows a great deal about Adolf Eichmann's escape from Europe after the war. While he was living in Argentina under the name of Ricardo Klement, Eichmann worked with the Dutch writer Willem Sassen to prepare a memoir of sorts. In it Eichmann talks extensively about his escape from Germany. After Israeli agents brought Eichmann to Israel in 1960, the authorities interrogated him rigorously. Historians have used these plentiful sources as well as earlier IWG declassifications.[15] The most recent American declassifications fill in some small gaps. They show what the West knew about Eichmann's criminality and his postwar movements. No American intelligence agency aided Eichmann's escape or simply allowed him to hide safely in Argentina.

Die Unklarheiten über die Zahl der getöteten Juden.

Anlässlich einer Unterhaltung mit SS-Obersturmbannführer Eichmann - etwa im Herbst 1944 - in Budapest erzählte mir dieser, dass er einen Bericht für Himmler machen musste mit genauen Zahlenangaben über die bisher getöteten Juden. Nachdem er selbst die eigentlichen Vernichtungskommandos nicht unter sich habe (was auch insoweit richtig ist, als Eichmann in ganz-Europa nur die Deportationen der Juden leitete bezw. organisierte) sei er auf Schätzungen angewiesen gewesen, wobei er zu der Zahl von 4 000 000 gekommen sei, die in den sogenannten Gaskammern und anderen systematischen Vernichtungsapparaturen umgekommen seien, während er die Zahl der darüber hinaus getöteten Juden auf etwa 2 000 000 veranschlug, wovon die Masse bei der Besetzung Polens und Russlands durch eigene Sonderkommandos den Tod durch Erschiessen fand. Himmler war mit diesem Bericht Eichmann's sehr unzufrieden und liess ihm mitteilen, dass er ihm den Leiter seines Statistischen Büros schicke, der aufgrund seiner Unterlagen das Material neu bearbeiten würde. Himmler liess bei seiner Antwort klar erkennen, dass ihm die Gesamtzahl von 6 000 000 ermordeter Juden zu gering sei und er in einem Bericht nachweisen wolle, dass die Zahl höher sein müsse.

The ambiguity over the number of Jews killed

On the occasion of a conversation with SS-Obersturmbannführer Eichmann - approximately in the autumn 1944 - in Budapest he told me that he had had to make a report for Himmler with the exact number of Jews killed thus far. Since he himself did not have the actual killing units (Vernichtungskommandos) subordinate to him (which is also to that extent correct, as Eichmann led and/or organized only the deportations of Jews throughout all of Europe), he was dependent on estimates, whereby he had come up with the number of 4,000,000 which died in the so-called gas chambers and other systematic means of destruction, while he determined that the number of the Jews killed above and beyond that at approximately 2,000,000, most of whom were shot during the occupation of Poland and Russia by the special detachments (Sonderkommandos). Himmler was very dissatisfied with Eichmann's report and he ordered that the records be sent to the head of his statistical office so that work could be started anew. Himmler's response clearly indicated that he believed that the total number of 6,000,000 murdered Jews was too low and that he wanted the report to prove the number must be higher.

In 1944, six months before the end of the war, Eichmann reported to Himmler on the exact number of Jews killed so far as 6,000,00—4,000,000 in the death camps and an additional 2,000,000 by the death squads in Poland and Russia. Hoettl reported Himmler was dissatisfied with the report, asserting the numbers must be higher. *RG 263, Records of the Central Intelligence Agency.*

Wartime information emanating from the anti-Nazi informant Fritz Kolbe tied Eichmann to the Theresienstadt camp and to the use of Hungarian Jews for slave labor.[16] In addition, Jewish sources had early postwar information about Eichmann, which they passed to the Allies, but much of it was of poor quality, reflecting myths that Eichmann or others close to him had spread. One July 1945 report called him Ingo Aichmann with an alias of Eichman, and claimed he had been born in Palestine in 1901. What Jewish officials knew was that Eichmann had arranged transport of Jews from Holland, Denmark, and Hungary.[17] This unevaluated report and others like it helped establish Eichmann's importance at a time when his name was little known among Allied authorities. Hungarian Jews who had survived, such as Rudolph Kastner, could have given plentiful information about Eichmann's activities in Hungary. But they had no idea where Eichmann was.

Gestapo official Rudolf Mildner noted Eichmann's skill as a mountaineer and gave the Army a list of his possible hiding places in the mountains: either in the Dachsteingebiet or the Steiermark and Salzburg area. The Army sent out an early October 1945 notice that it wanted Eichmann urgently for interrogation and possibly for trial as a war criminal.[18]

In late October 1945, OSS sources indicated to the Army that Eichmann might be hiding in the Steiermark or Salzburg areas. Special Agent John H. Richardson asked local Austrian police in Salzburg to arrest Eichmann and turn him over to the CIC.[19] Although the CIC in Austria had no files on Eichmann of its own, it passed along sketchy, mostly accurate information from Supreme Headquarters Allied Expeditionary Forces files.[20] The Research Office of the United Nations War Crimes Commission issued an October 1945 report on Eichmann that reached the Judge Advocate General's office. It contained some detail about Eichmann's wartime activities.[21]

In November 1945 the Counter-Intelligence War Room in London issued the first substantial Allied intelligence report on Eichmann, drawn from interrogations of a number of captured Nazi officials who had known him. It offered a physical description and a reasonable account of his career, calling him a war criminal of the highest importance. It included what he had told other Nazis about the number of Jews murdered by the Nazis and places he and others might hide if the war were lost. The report gave details about Eichmann's family and revealed the identity of one of his mistresses.[22]

Today we know that near the end of the war Eichmann had gone to the village of Altaussee in Austria. On May 2 he had met with his superior, Ernst Kaltenbrunner. More or less according to Kaltenbrunner's instructions—Kaltenbrunner probably did not want to be caught with Eichmann—he then retreated into the mountains to hide. But then he left. After a visit to Salzburg, he tried to slip across the border to Bavaria. American forces arrested him, apparently in late May. At first, he used the identity of a corporal named Barth, but after his SS tattoo was recognized and U.S. Army officers poked holes in his story, he transformed himself into Otto Eckmann, a second lieutenant in the Waffen-SS. The Army soon sent him to a POW camp at Weiden, where he stayed until August 1945. Then he was moved to another POW camp at Ober-Dachstetten in Franconia. Some Jewish survivors came to this camp to pick out known war criminals, but Eichmann managed to avoid recognition. (The Army established a file on an Otto Eckmann, but it is one of a small percentage of IRR digital files that cannot be retrieved.) While the Counter-Intelligence War Room alerted Allied forces in Europe about Eichmann's importance, he was hiding under a pseudonym at an American camp.[23]

In January 1946 the CIC recognized that Eichmann was partly responsible for the extermination of six million Jews, requested his immediate apprehension, and suggested close surveillance of his mistress, who owned a small paper factory in a village in the Austrian Alps.[24] Renewed war crimes interrogations of Eichmann's associate Wilhelm Höttl and Eichmann's subordinate Dieter Wisliceny convinced prosecutors that Eichmann was still alive. They asked the CIC to search for him in and around Salzburg. The CIC did so, but he was long gone from the region.[25]

In December 1945 the International Military Tribunal at Nuremberg had raised the subject of the Nazi extermination of Jews. American prosecutors presented and discussed an affidavit by Wilhelm Höttl, who said Eichmann had told him that the Nazis killed approximately six million Jews—the first time this statistic had appeared. A major article in the *New York Times* brought the name Adolf Eichmann to millions of people.[26] Then Eichmann's subordinate Dieter Wisliceny testified in-depth, adding much detail about Eichmann and his office.[27]

Hearing about the publicity about him, Eichmann decided to break out of the American camp and reinvent himself as Otto Henninger, a businessman. He ended up in the British zone of Germany, where he leased some land and raised chickens. By the late 1940s the British had no interest in further war crimes trials. But when Eichmann heard that Nazi war crimes hunter Simon Wiesenthal had instigated a raid on his wife's home in Austria in 1950, he decided to make use of old SS contacts to go to Argentina.[28]

In 1952 the Austrian police chief in Salzburg asked the CIC whether it still sought Eichmann's arrest. An official of the 430th CIC detachment in Austria noted that Wiesenthal, described as an Israeli intelligence operative, was hunting Eichmann and was offering a large reward. In a memo to Assistant Chief of Staff, G-2, the CIC noted that its mission no longer included the apprehension of war criminals, and "it is also believed that the prosecution of war criminals is no longer considered of primary interest to U.S. Authorities." On these grounds, the Army should advise the Salzburg police that Eichmann was no longer sought. But in view of Eichmann's reputation and the interest of other countries [Israel] in apprehending him, it might be a mistake to show lack of interest. So the CIC recommended confirming continuing U.S. interest in Eichmann.[29]

In 1953 New Jersey Senator H. Alexander Smith acting on behalf of Rabbi Abraham Kalmanowitz, a leading figure in the Orthodox Jewish rescue organization known as Vaad Ha-Hatzalah, asked the CIA to make an effort to find Eichmann. Kalmanowitz viewed him as a threat to world peace. The memorandum by the Chief of CIA's Near East and Africa Division, subunit-2, was cleared by CIA General Counsel Larry Houston and stated: "while CIA has a continuing interest in the whereabouts and activities of individuals such as Eichmann, we are not in the business of apprehending war criminals, hence in no position to take an active role in this case; that we would, however, be alert for any information regarding Eichmann's whereabouts and pass it on to appropriate authorities (probably the West German Government) for such action as may be indicated."[30]

By then, contradictory rumors speculated that Eichmann was currently in Egypt, Argentina, or Jerusalem, and falsely ascribing his place of birth to the latter city. Some CIA reports unknowingly confused Adolf Karl Eichmann with Karl

Heinz Eichmann, who reportedly was in Cairo or Damascus. Indistinguishable among these false rumors assembled by West German intelligence was unconfirmed but accurate information concerning a "Clemens" in Argentina.[31]

In March 2010 the international press noted that the German intelligence service, the BND, had a classified file of some 4,500 pages of documents on Eichmann, purportedly about Eichmann's escape to Italy and then Argentina.[32] American IRR records and CIA records on Eichmann may supplement or serve as a check on these German files once they are released.

NOTES

1　The effort by British intelligence is covered in Hugh Trevor Roper, *The Last Days of Hitler* (New York: Macmillan, 1947), and subsequent reprints. The Soviet effort is discussed in Henrik Eberle and Matthias Uhl, ed., *The Hitler Book: The Secret Dossier Prepared for Stalin from the Interrogation of Hitler's Personal Aides* (New York: Public Affairs, 2005).

2　Michael A. Mussmano Collection, Duquesne University Archives and Special Collections, Pittsburgh, PA, FF 25, Folder 32.

3　The English translation is Melissa Müller, ed., *Until the Final Hour: Hitler's Last Secretary* (New York: Arcade, 2004).

4　Memorandum for the Officer in Charge, Junge, Gertaud, June 13, 1946, NARA, RG 319, IRR Junge, Traudl, XA 085512.For Kempka's testimony, see International Military Tribunal *Trial of the Major War Criminals before the International Military Tribunal, Nuremberg, 14 November 1945 –1 October 1946* (Nuremberg: IMT, 1946), vol. 17 (hereafter *TMWC*), pp. 446ff.

5　Richard Overy, *Interrogations: The Nazi Elite in Allied Hands* (New York: Viking, 2001), pp. 113–14.

6　Memorandum for the Officer in Charge, Junge, Gertraud, Interrogation Report No. 2, June 18, 1946, NARA, RG 319, IRR Junge, Traudl, XA 085512. The account of her escape here is at odds in many respects with that given in 2001 to Melissa Müller, See Müller, ed., *Final Hour*, pp. 219–27.

7　Memorandum for the Officer in Charge, August 30, 1946, Interrogation of Junge, Gertraud, NARA, RG 319, IRR, Junge, Traudl, XA 085512.

8　Timothy Naftali, Norman J.W. Goda, Richard Breitman, Robert Wolfe, "The Mystery of Heinrich Müller: New Materials from the CIA," *Holocaust and Genocide Studies*, v. 15, n. 3 (Winter 2001): 453–67.

9　Memorandum for the Officer in Charge, August 30, 1946, Interrogation of Junge, Gertraud, NARA, RG 319, IRR, Junge, Traudl, XA 085512.

10　Peter Black, *Ernst Kaltenbrunner: Ideological Soldier of the Third Reich* (Princeton, NJ: Princeton University Press, 1984), pp. 244–52.

11　Figure in Patrick Montague, *Chelmno and the Holocaust: A History of Hitler's First Death Camp* (London: I. B. Tauris, 2011).

12　On Greiser, see Catherine Epstein, *Model Nazi: Arthur Greiser and the Occupation of Western*

Poland (New York: Oxford University Press, 2010); and Alexander V. Prusin, "Poland's Nuremberg: The Seven Court Cases of Poland's Supreme National Tribunal," *Holocaust and Genocide Studies*, vol. 24, no. 1 (2010): 1-25. We are grateful to Epstein and Prusin for their assistance. Epstein contributed to this section of our report.

13 Files relating to Greiser's materials amount to 2,126 pages in all. See NARA, RG 319, IRR Greiser, Arthur, XE 000933A; NARA, RG 319, IRR Greiser, Arthus: Contents of Notebooks, XE 000933.

14 Greiser's biographer Epstein, professor of history at Amherst College, had seen other copies of some of these documents in other archives; however, she had never before seen a substantial part of this evidence.

15 In just the last few years British historian David Cesarani has written a scholarly biography of Eichmann, and writer Neil Bascomb has described in colorful detail the Allied and Israeli search for Eichmann. David Cesarani *Becoming Eichmann: Rethinking the Life, Crimes and Trial of a "Desk Murderer"* (New York: De Capo Press, 2006); Neil Bascomb, *Hunting Eichmann: How a Band of Survivors and a Young Spy Agency Chased Down the World's Most Notorious Nazi* (New York: Houghton Mifflin, 2009).

16 The Benzberg and Theresienstadt Concentration Camps, and Conscripted Jewish Labor from Hungary, NARA, RG 226, Entry 210, Box 432, WN# 16464 and 16460.

17 Ingo Eichman, July 27, 1945, NARA RG 153, E 144, B 83. This document was declassified long ago.

18 Headquarters USFET Military Intelligence Service Center, September 25, 1945, re: Eichmann, Adolf, NARA, RG 319, IRR Mildner, Dr. Rudolf, D 00880; Sassard Memo re: Eichmann, Adolf, October 9, 1945, NARA, RG 319, IRR Eichmann, Karl Adolf, XE 004471.

19 This document is reprinted in Bundespolizeidirektion Salzburg to CIC, March 24, 1952, NARA, RG 319, IRR Eichmann, Karl Adolf, XE 004471.

20 NARA, RG 319, IRR Eichmann, Karl Adolf, XE 004471.

21 Material Related to SS-Obersturmbannführer Adolf Eichmann, October 1945, NARA, RG 153, E 144, B 90.

22 Werner Goettsch, Wilhelm Höttl, Kurt Auner, and Wilhelm Waneck were the main sources. Counter Intelligence War Room, London to Major Stewart, November 19, 1945, NARA, RG 319, IRR Eichmann, Adolf MSN 52577.

23 Bascomb, *Hunting Eichmann*, 19–23, 37–38, 42–43; Cesarani, *Becoming Eichmann*, 202–3.

24 CIC Central Registry, Summary of Information, January 10, 1946, NARA, RG 319, IRR Eichmann, Adolf, MSN 52577.

25 Office of Chief of Counsel to Maj. Thomas K. Hodges, CIC, March 21, 1946; Robert J. Brown, Special Agent, CIC to Officer in Charge, June 27, 1946, re: Eichmann, Adolf, NARA, RG 319, IRR Eichmann, Adolf, MSN 52577.

26 "Trial Data Reveal 6,000,000 Jews Died," *New York Times*, December 15, 1945, p. 8.

27 *TMWC*, v. 4, pp. 354ff.

28 Cesarani, *Becoming Eichmann*, 203–205.

29 Disposition Form, Eichmann, Adolf, March 31, 1952, NARA, RG 319, IRR Eichmann, Karl Adolf, XE 004471.

30 Berle to Dulles, September 28, 1953; Kalmanowitz to Dulles, September 30, 1953; NE-2 to Dulles, October 20, 1953, NARA, RG 263, E ZZ-19, B 30, Adolf Eichmann Name File, vol. 2, part 1.

31 This section on the CIA's knowledge of Eichmann is adapted from a longer report by Robert Wolfe, "Did the CIA Really Cold-Shoulder the Hunt for Adolf Eichmann?" National Archives Research Papers, *www.archives.gov/iwg/research-papers/eichmann.html*.

32 *www.spiegel.de/international/germany/0,1518,682826,00.html*.

German financial support of Arab leaders during the entire war was astonishing. The Grand Mufti Amin el Husseini and Raschid Ali El Gailani financed their operations with funding from the German Foreign Ministry from 1941–45. German intention in the Arab countries was based on an expectation of establishing pro-German governments in the Middle East. *RG 319, Records of the Army Staff.*

CHAPTER TWO

Nazis and the Middle East

Recent scholarship has highlighted Nazi aims in the Middle East, including the intent to murder the Jewish population of Palestine with a special task force that was to accompany the Afrika Korps past the Suez Canal in the summer of 1942.[1] Scholars have also re-examined the relationship between the Nazi state and Haj Amin al-Husseini, the Grand Mufti of Jerusalem, as well as the postwar place of the Holocaust in Arab and Muslim thinking.[2] Newly released CIC and CIA records supplement this scholarship in revealing ways.

Einsatzkommando Egypt

The 1946 testimony of Franz Hoth casts interesting light on both Nazi territorial objectives and Jewish policy in 1940–42. British troops in Norway captured Hoth, an SS and Sicherheitsdienst (Security Service or SD) officer who had served in a number of different mobile killing units called Einsatzkommandos.[3] When in March 1946 British interrogators asked Hoth about the functions of the Einsatzkommandos, he studiously avoided giving self-incriminating statements. His interrogator seems to have liked him: "Hoth declares—and the interrogator is inclined to believe him—that throughout his SD career, he tried to work in accordance with his ideals. It is not thought that Hoth would consciously have made himself guilty of any crimes…."[4] As a result of this generous assessment, his interrogator let him get away with many evasive answers.

Nevertheless, Hoth gave useful background about the early 1941 training of police officers slated for deployment in Africa when Germany expected to establish a raw materials empire there. At the Security Police School in Berlin-Charlottenburg, medical experts, Foreign Office officials, and other experts lectured to three classes of about 30 police officers each; additional classes were held for non-commissioned officers. "The purpose of these courses was to make the students familiar with the history and problems of the former German colonies in preparation for the day when these colonies would be retrieved by Germany," Hoth explained. Afterwards, all the German police officers went to Rome (April 1941), attending an Italian police school where they learned how the Italian police handled resistance in the Italian African colonies.[5]

Hoth was friendly with a senior official of the Reich Security Main Office (RSHA) named Walter Rauff, one of the inventors and distributors of the gas van used to asphyxiate victims in Belarus and later at the Chelmno extermination camp. Because of his connection with Rauff, who was slated for command of an Einsatzkommando in North Africa, and his colonial training, Hoth was appointed head of section I of Rauff's Einsatzkommando Egypt, which was assembled and dispatched to Athens in July 1942. There the unit waited for General Rommel's troops to conquer Egypt and move into the British-controlled Mandate of Palestine, where roughly half a million Jews lived.[6]

Rauff's Einsatzkommando, technically subordinated to Rommel's army, reported directly to the RSHA in Berlin. After Reinhard Heydrich was assassinated in Czechoslovakia, SS chief Heinrich Himmler took direct command of this umbrella security-police organization. Two German historians have indicated that Himmler conferred with Hitler about the deployment of Einsatzkommando Egypt, which was to take "executive measures" against civilians on its own authority, in other words, the mass murder of Jews.[7] In 1946 Hoth commented only that his Einsatzkommando was supposed to perform the usual Security Police and SD duties in Egypt; he avoided saying that such duties elsewhere had included the mass execution of Jews. But this context puts a rather different light on what his British interrogator called Hoth's idealism.

Hitler himself signaled his intention to eliminate the Jews of Palestine. In a November 28, 1941, conversation in Berlin with Haj Amin al-Husseini, the Grand Mufti of Jerusalem, Hitler said that the outcome of the war in Europe would also decide the fate of the Arab world. German troops intended to break through the Caucasus region and move into the Middle East. This would result in the liberation of Arab peoples. Hitler said that Germany's only objective there would be the destruction of the Jews.[8]

The British never prosecuted Hoth for his Einsatzkommando activities. But he had also served in the Security Police in the French city of Nancy, and the French military authorities found him guilty of crimes there. He was sentenced to death and executed in 1949.[9]

New Documentation: Haj Amin al-Husseini's Contract

Recent books have added greatly to our knowledge of Haj Amin al-Husseini's activities as leader of anti-Jewish revolts in the British Mandate in Palestine in 1929 and 1936, as the impetus behind the pro-German coup in Iraq in April 1941, and as a pro-Nazi propagandist in Berlin, broadcasting over German short-wave radio to large audiences in the Middle East starting in late 1941.[10] CIA and U.S. Army files on Husseini offer small pieces of new evidence about his relationship with the Nazi government and his escape from postwar justice.

The Nazi government financed Husseini and Rashid Ali el-Gailani, the former premier of Iraq who had joined Husseini in Berlin after his failed coup in Iraq. After the war Carl Berthold Franz Rekowski, an official of the German Foreign Office who had dealt with Husseini, testified that the Foreign Office financially supported the two Arab leaders, their families, and other Arabs in their entourage who had fled to Germany after the coup. Husseini and Gailani determined how these funds were distributed among the others. The CIA file on Husseini includes a document indicating that he had a staff of 20–30 men in Berlin. A separate source indicates that he lived in a villa in the Krumme Lanke neighborhood of Berlin. From spring 1943 to spring 1944, Husseini personally received 50,000 marks monthly and Gailani 65,000 for operational expenses. In addition, they each received living expenses averaging 80,000 marks per month, an absolute fortune. A German field marshal received a base salary of 26,500 marks per year.[11] Finally, Husseini and Gailani received substantial foreign currency to support adherents living in countries outside Germany.[12]

Through conversations with other Foreign Office officials, Rekowski learned that Nazi authorities planned to use both Arab leaders to control their respective countries after Germany conquered them. Gailani was an Iraqi nationalist who maintained good ties with the German Foreign Office. Husseini, however, was a believer in a Pan-Arab state. His closest ties were with the SS. The other Arabs were divided into one camp or the other.

SS-Sturmbannführer Wilhelm Beisner, like Hoth, an officer on Einsatzkommando Egypt, had frequent contact with Husseini during the war.[13] Beisner told Rekowski that Husseini had good ties with Himmler and with Waffen-SS Gen. Gottlob Berger, who handled the recruitment of non-German forces into the Waffen-SS. SS leaders and Husseini both claimed that Nazism and Islam had common values as well as common enemies—above all, the Jews.[14]

Another independent source of information on Husseini's ties with the SS was the disaffected and abused wife of a young Egyptian, Dr. Abdel Halim el-Naggar, who had worked in Berlin for the German Foreign Office and the Propaganda Ministry. An Egyptian named Galal in Berlin edited an Arabic-language periodical designed to stir up the Arabs to support Germany, and el-Naggar assisted him in 1940. By 1941 el-Naggar had his own Arabic publication for Middle Eastern audiences, and in 1942 he took on the additional job of director of Nazi short-wave broadcasts to the Near East. After Husseini came to Berlin, he wanted to cooperate with el-Naggar on Middle Eastern broadcasts, and for a time they worked together successfully. Then el-Naggar established an Islamic Central Institute in Berlin. Husseini had wanted to head this institute, and after el-Naggar refused him, Husseini used his influence with the SS to get el-Naggar removed from the broadcasting job.[15]

In the fall of 1943 Husseini went to the Independent State of Croatia, a Nazi ally, to recruit Muslims for the Waffen-SS. During that trip he told the troops of the newly formed Bosnian-Muslim 13th Mountain Waffen-SS division that the entire Muslim world ought to follow their example. Husseini also organized a 1944 mission for Palestinian Arabs and Germans to carry out sabotage and propaganda after German planes dropped them into Palestine by parachute. In discussions with the Foreign Intelligence branch of the RSHA, Husseini insisted that the Arabs take command after they landed and direct their fight against the Jews of Palestine, not the British authorities.[16]

Today we have more detailed scholarly accounts today of Husseini's war-time activities, but Husseini's CIA file indicates that wartime Allied intelligence organizations gathered a healthy portion of this incriminating evidence. This evidence is significant in light of Husseini's lenient postwar treatment.[17]

In the spring of 1945, a German Foreign Office official reached agreement with Gailani effective April 1: his cash payments were raised to 85,000 marks, but Gailani would repay the Germans after his forces reconquered Iraq. Similarly, according to a newly declassified document, the Foreign Office and Husseini signed a contract for subsidies of up to 12,000 marks per month to continue after April 1, 1945, with the Mufti pledging to repay these amounts later. In April 1945 neither side could have had much doubt about the outcome of the war. The continuing contractual relationships meant that Nazi officials and the two Arab leaders hoped to continue their joint or complementary political-ideological campaign in the postwar period.[18]

Declassified CIA and Army files establish that the Allies knew enough about Husseini's wartime activities to consider him a war criminal. Apparently fearing Allied prosecution,[19] he tried to flee to Switzerland at the end of the war. Swiss authorities turned him over to the French, who brought him to Paris.

Haj Amin al-Husseini's Escape

Right after the war ended a group of Palestinian-Arab soldiers in the British Army who were stationed in Lebanon had staged anti-French demonstrations. They carried around a large picture of Husseini and declared him to be the "sword of the faith."[20] According to one source considered reliable by the rump American intelligence organization known as the Strategic Services Unit (SSU), British officials objected to French plans to prosecute Husseini, fearing that this would cause political unrest in Palestine. The British "threatened" the French with Arab uprisings in French Morocco.[21]

In October 1945 Arthur Giles (who used the title Bey), British head of Palestine's Criminal Investigation Division, told the assistant American military attaché in Cairo that the Mufti might be the only person who could unite the Palestine Arabs and "cool off the Zionists.... Of course, we can't do it, but it might not be such a damn bad idea at that." French intelligence officials, bitter at France's loss of colonial territory in the Middle East, said they would enjoy having the Mufti around to embarrass the British.[22]

Husseini was well treated in Paris. Meanwhile, Palestinian Arab leaders and various Muslim extremists agitated to bring him back to the Middle East. According to the American military attaché in Cairo, this plan initially embarrassed moderate officials in the Arab League. But as prospects for a peaceful settlement in the British Mandate for Palestine declined and as other Arab prisoners were released or escaped (Gailani escaped), sentiment changed. A delegate of the Palestine Higher Arab Committee went to Paris in June 1946 and told Husseini to get ready for a little trip.[23]

According to another American source in Syria, at a meeting in the Egyptian Embassy in Paris, the ambassador, the ministers of Syria and Lebanon, and a few Arab leaders from Morocco and Algeria worked out the details of Husseini's escape. The French government learned of, or was informed of, the plan, but chose not to intervene in order to avoid offending the Arabs of North Africa. Husseini flew to Syria, then went via Aleppo and Beirut to Alexandria, Egypt.[24]

By 1947 Husseini denied that he had worked for the Axis powers during the war. He told one acquaintance that he hoped soon to have documentary evidence rebutting this slander, which the Jews were spreading. Similarly, after Adolf Eichmann was brought to Israel for trial in March 1961, Husseini, by now in Beirut, denied having ever met Eichmann during the war. He said that he had been forced to take refuge in Germany simply because British wanted to capture him. Nazi persecution of Jews had served Zionism, according to Husseini, by exciting world sympathy for them. Husseini never worked for American intelligence; the CIA simply considered him a person worth tracking. He died in Beirut in 1974.[25]

Wilhelm Beisner, Franz Rademacher, and Alois Brunner

The CIA and the CIC both compiled files on the versatile and French-speaking Wilhelm Beisner, who dealt with Husseini during and after the war. It is possible to trace Beisner's long intelligence career better than has been done before. His tracks after the war intersected with those of German Foreign Office deportation specialist Franz Rademacher, and Adolf Eichmann's subordinate Alois Brunner. All three spent most of their postwar years in the Middle East.

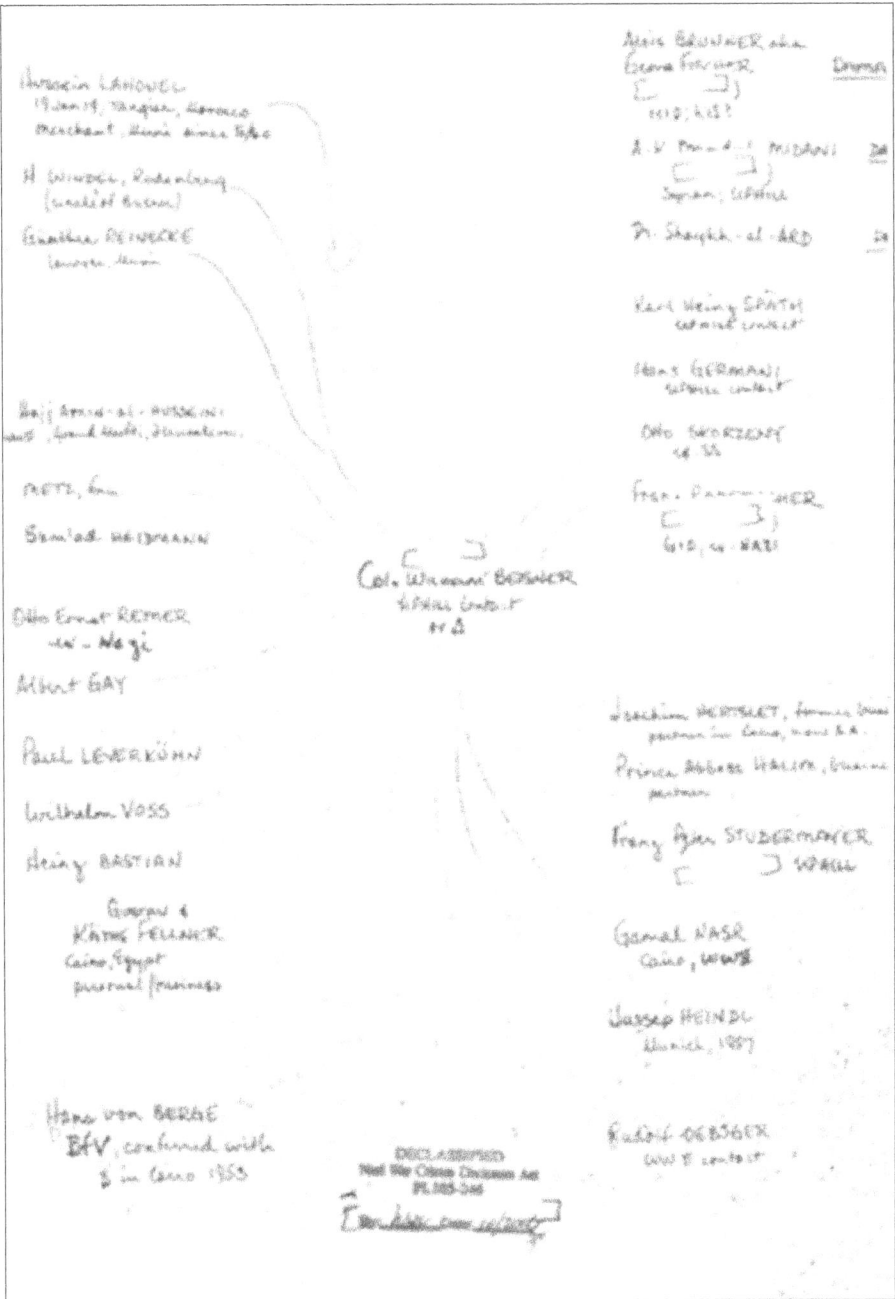

The CIA diagram shows a nexus of former Nazis—Beisner, Skorzeny, Rademacher, Brunner and Remer — with important Arab leaders—the Grand Mufti Hajj Amin el Husseini, Abbass Halim, and Gamal Nasser. *RG 263, Central Intelligence Agency.*

Franz Rademacher—linked to the persecution of Jews—fled first to Spain and then to Syria, It is believed that Hans Globke, Adenauer's personal aide, assisted his escape. *RG 319, Records of the Army Staff.*

In April 1945 an unnamed German defected to Switzerland and offered up Beisner as a war criminal of Allied interest. Although Allen Dulles's office did not trust the informant, they rated his information good.[26] According to this report, Beisner trained as an agronomist, then went into Alfred Rosenberg's Nazi Party Foreign Policy Office (Aussenpolitisches Amt), becoming a specialist in the Balkan region. He was allegedly involved in the Iron Guard's unsuccessful January 1941 coup in Bucharest—a Romanian "Kristallnacht" in which 120 Jews were brutally murdered. The informant mistakenly placed Beisner as head of the Gestapo in Lodz and Zagreb. Beisner did, however, serve a term in the Waffen-SS, where he was assigned to the Selbstschutz, a "self-defense" force of ethnic Germans used to carry out brutal and murderous policies in German-occupied Polish territory.[27] Although his SS personnel file lacks evidence of it, from the spring of 1941 until late that year he served in Croatia as head of an Einsatzkommando Zagreb (part of Einsatzgruppe Yugoslavia). Croatian sources list him also as German police attaché to the new Independent State of Croatia.[28]

The Ustaschi government in Croatia admired the SS and was eager to win Himmler's favor, according to the Croatian minister in Berlin.[29] The period Beisner was in Croatia was precisely the period when the Croatian Ustaschi engaged in massive killings of Jews and Serbs. In January 1942 Beisner received the German war cross of merit, second class, for his service, and in 1943 the Croatian government decorated him as well.[30]

At the end of 1941 Beisner joined SD Foreign Intelligence as a specialist in the Middle East. Assigned as an officer to Einsatzkommando Egypt, he went to Athens to await Rommel's conquest of Egypt.[31] After Rommel's defeat, he then shifted to Tunis, where he commanded a Security Police and SD unit and served as liaison to the Grand Mufti.[32] He also set up an intelligence network in Tunis, which French intelligence sources reported on in some detail. When German forces had to evacuate Tunisia, Beisner went to Italy, and he tried to keep his Tunisian network running. In fact, he sought intelligence covering the Near East generally.[33]

He spent the last part of the war in Italy, where American forces apparently captured him. Gehlen Organization sources later said Beisner escaped from American internment with French help and then went to work for French intelligence in Austria.[34] In late 1950 an Austrian official who located Beisner in Munich asked the CIA for information about him. A CIA official thought Austrian interest stemmed from their belief that Beisner was working for West German intelligence. The CIA post in Karlsruhe reported that Beisner had a business enterprise in Munich named Omnia that probably served as cover for French intelligence activities.[35]

A West German intelligence report in March 1952 indicated that Beisner had been involved in black-market arms transactions among Switzerland, Spain, and France. Discovery of these activities forced him to go to Cairo, where he allegedly continued to work for the French and enjoyed good connections with the Americans as well. (CIA did not think much of that last comment.) He seems to have been active in purchasing arms for the Egyptian government.[36] Another CIA document indicated that Beisner arrived in Cairo on July 21, 1951, as representative of a Hamburg firm called Terramar and that he offered his services to the Gehlen Organization.[37]

By then other Germans had arrived in Egypt. In December 1952 the West German ambassador to Egypt, speaking to the press in Bonn, drew a clear distinction between German military advisers in Egypt and former Nazis in certain Middle Eastern countries linked with Haj Amin al-Husseini; these Nazis were working to impair relations between Arab states and West Germany, incite disturbances, and spread chaos.[38]

In Cairo, Beisner did resume contact with Haj Amin al-Husseini. Al-Husseini helped him get a visa for a Polish Jew named Hertslett, who worked with Beisner in the Egyptian Continental Trading Company, a firm involved in arms deals and illicit traffic. According to information CIA received through an Italian business contact of Beisner, Prime Minister Najib of Egypt used Beisner to negotiate a large purchase of machine guns and cannons, which were to be routed through Spain if the United States did not object.[39] Later that year, the economic section of the American Embassy in Egypt warned that the Egyptian Continental Trading Company had a bad reputation. Beisner and Hertslett had tried to pass themselves off as working on behalf of the West German government to foster trade between West Germany and Egypt; they were now blacklisted and had little means.[40] The CIA had no direct contact with Beisner. Most of the CIA's information about his Egyptian activities originated with the Gehlen Organization.[41]

In 1954 the CIC received a report that Beisner was running Egyptian intelligence operations for an organization called the Institute for Contemporary Research (Institut für Gegenwartsforschung). This institute was likely connected with a shadowy West German intelligence organization run by Friedrich Wilhelm Heinz called the Amt Blank. The CIC checked Beisner's SS Personnel records at the Berlin Document Center, but they were fragmentary.[42]

Beisner's importance grew in February 1958 when Franz Rademacher, living in Damascus under a pseudonym, told an unnamed CIA source in Syria that Gamal Abdel Nasser (called Jamal Nasir in one document and Gamal Nasir in another) had worked for the Germans during the war, and that Beisner had served as his liaison. They still were close, Rademacher claimed.[43]

After leading a revolution and becoming the second president of Egypt in 1956, Nasser had established an intelligence organization under Zakaria Mohieddin. Zakaria had chosen Beisner's former RSHA comrade Joachim Deumling as his intelligence adviser. Deumling had worked for the British Army of the Rhine after the war, but the British blacklisted him for security reasons in 1951.[44] When he decided to leave West Germany for Egypt, he traveled secretly to avoid attracting British attention. Zakaria, who soon became minister of the interior as well, praised Deumling's intelligence work in Egypt.[45]

Beisner may have benefited from an increasing presence of former Nazis in Cairo under Nasser. He later claimed that while in Cairo he had helped to train Algerian volunteers for the struggle to liberate Algeria from French control and that he sold arms to the Algerian National Liberation Front.[46] Whether he operated on his own or with Egyptian intelligence approval is unclear.

In March 1958 an unnamed CIA source contacted Beisner through Rademacher in Syria nominally to get assistance on a possible contract to build radar stations in Saudi Arabia. Impressed with Beisner's acumen, the man asked the CIA if it would like him to pursue a business relationship with Beisner. CIA officials saw a number of unanswered questions about Beisner and concluded that the source could pursue a business relationship with him without any Agency involvement.[47]

Rademacher's own route to the Middle East was convoluted. In 1952 West German authorities had lodged charges against Rademacher for his involvement in the murder and deportation of Jews in several countries. Although acquitted of many of the charges in spite of substantial evidence against him, he was sentenced to three years for his role in arranging deportations of Jews from Serbia and eight months for being an accessory to similar activity in Belgium. After West German authorities released him on bail during his appeal, he went into hiding, eventually fleeing to Spain and then Syria.[48] In 1957 Rademacher hinted to a right-wing German with good contacts in Syria that Konrad Adenauer's aide Hans Globke, with whom Rademacher had worked during the war, had assisted his flight from West Germany. He also claimed a good connection with the chief of Syrian intelligence. His formal position in Damascus was partner in the import-export firm of Souheb Mahmoudy, and he used the name of a Spaniard, Bartolomé Rossello. The CIC source mentioned Rademacher's contacts with a "Beischner" and an "Otto Fischer," about whom Rademacher was unwilling to say much.[49]

By 1959 the CIA had tentatively concluded that Beisner was a source for West German intelligence. A high BND official codenamed Winterstein conceded that the BND had a loose relationship with Beisner, meaning it had contact with him, but could not really direct him or his activities. But the BND kept in mind that, given his frequent travels and contacts, it was likely Beisner had a close connection with Egyptian intelligence.[50]

In October 1960, while in Munich, where his wife kept an apartment, Beisner was wounded when a bomb exploded in his car. West German police speculated that the French terrorist organization called the Red Hand had carried out the attack. A BND official told CIA that, in his personal opinion, Beisner worked for Egyptian intelligence, and that the Red Hand had arranged the explosion. Beisner's vision was damaged, and he lost a leg. Today, we know that the Red Hand was a unit sponsored by the French Intelligence (Documentation and External Counterespionage Service or SDECE) to carry out assassinations and attacks against the Algerian liberation movement.[51]

By then, Beisner had fallen into disfavor in Egypt, possibly because of general distrust of foreigners, or more likely because of dissatisfaction with how he had handled commissions on his arms deals.[52] As a result of his difficulties, Beisner wrote a man using the name Georg Fischer or Rischer in Damascus to see whether he would be welcome in Syria. In his handwritten reply, "Rischer" said that his friends would be happy to talk with Beisner face-to-face, and he himself would be pleased to see Beisner. "Rischer" also complained about a recent article that slandered Egypt, Syria, and their leading officials. He said it very much resembled Zionist propaganda against Nazi Germany after 1936![53]

An intelligence agency intercepted the mail to Alice Beisner's Munich apartment and passed copies to the CIA. (Although the BND said that it was a French intercept operation, the CIA thought that the BND itself might have done it.) As a result, the CIA read "Rischer's" reply. CIA officials concluded, after comparing handwriting, that Rischer was really Alois Brunner, Adolf Eichmann's onetime subordinate, who was now serving as an adviser to Syrian intelligence. In subsequent correspondence Rischer strongly recommended that Beisner read Simon Wiesenthal's new book *I Hunted Eichmann*.[54]

CIA officials received other indications that Fischer/Rischer was Brunner.[55] A CIA official in Munich had an informal discussion in March 1961 with a BND official codenamed Glueckrath, who claimed that a grand council of the Egyptian SS group had met several times in late 1960 and January 1961. Brunner had attended, along with Fritz Katzmann, former Higher SS and Police Leader in Galicia, who had gone into hiding at the end of the war and escaped justice. Other participants named were former Nazi propagandist Johannes von Leers, a major from Egyptian intelligence, and a lieutenant colonel from the Egyptian Ministry of Information. At this meeting Brunner claimed to possess a long list of Jews who had collaborated with the Nazis during the Final Solution; they could now be blackmailed to help finance the SS group. Von Leers said that if this blackmail failed, he at least wanted to publish the list.[56]

Beisner ended up resettling in Tunis, not Damascus. CIA last traced him there in 1966, still wheeling and dealing. Rademacher was put on the payroll of the West German Secret Service sometime in 1961 or early 1962. The CIA was aware of Rademacher's status with the BND and interested in his activities, but had no direct contact with him.[57]

After France intercepted a shipment of arms to Algerian liberation forces, Rademacher was suspected of having leaked the information. Syrian authorities arrested him for spying. Thrown into prison, he was released in 1965 because of poor health—he had suffered two heart attacks in prison. He decided to return to West Germany in September 1966, where he was tried again, convicted, and given a five-year sentence. However, the judges gave him more than full credit for time served in American internment after the war. He died as a free man in 1973.[58] Alois Brunner survived an assassination attempt and remained in Syria—the last member of Adolf Eichmann's team. He apparently died there in 1992.[59]

Beisner, Rademacher, Brunner, Deumling, and a number of other former SS and police officials found not only havens, but postwar employment in Middle Eastern countries. There they were able to carry on and transmit to others Nazi racial-ideological anti-Semitism. Beisner, Rademacher, and particularly Brunner played important roles in the systematic killing of millions of Jews, and they continued to fulminate about Jewish influence decades later.

Much of the evidence of their postwar influence in Middle Eastern countries comes from their own statements. Driven by Nazi obsessions, these men never had a clear grasp of objective political realities, and they may also have exaggerated their postwar influence. Others who talked about them are far from perfect sources. Still, these intelligence reports, cross-checked against each other, are all the documentary sources we have about them. Perhaps one day the opening of archives in Middle Eastern countries will allow further insight into how far their influence went.

NOTES

1 Klaus-Michael Mallmann and Martin Cüppers, *Nazi Palestine: The Plans for the Extermination of the Jews of Palestine* (New York: Enigma Press, 2010).

2 Jeffrey Herf, *Nazi Propaganda for the Arab World* (New Haven: Yale University Press, 2009).

3 On Hoth's career, see Report on Interrogation of SS-Sturmbannführer Franz Hoth, March 15, 1946, PWIS (Norway)/81, NARA, RG 319, IRR Hoth, Franz, D 033387. This file is newly declassified in the United States but may have been available in the United Kingdom and Germany earlier.

4 Report on Interrogation of SS-Stubaf. Franz Hoth, March 15, 1946, PWIS (Norway)/81, NARA, RG 319, IRR Hoth, Franz, D 033387.

5 Interrogation of Hoth, March 15, 1946/PWIS (Norway)/83, NARA, RG 319, IRR Hoth, Franz, D 033387.

6 Mallmann and Cüppers, *Nazi Palestine*, pp. 117–18.

7 Mallmann and Cüppers, *Nazi Palestine*, pp. 117–18.

8 See discussion in Jeffrey Herf, *Nazi Propaganda for the Arab World*, pp. 76–78, and Mallmann and Cüppers, *Nazi Palestine*, pp. 89–91.

9 Mallmann and Cüppers, *Nazi Palestine*, p. 206.

10 Herf, *Nazi Propaganda*, passim; Klaus Gensicke, *Der Mufti von Jerusalem und die Nationalsozialisten* (Darmstadt: Wissenschaftliche Buchgesellschaft. 2007); Hillel Cohen, *Army of Shadows: Palestinian Collaboration with Zionism, 1917–1948* (Berkeley: University of California Press, 2008).

11 See Norman J.W. Goda, "Black Marks: Hitler's Bribery of His Senior Military Officers," *Journal of Modern History*, v. 72, n. 2 (June 2000): 413–52.

12 Final Interrogation Report of Rekowski, August 23, 1945, Annex III, August 14, 1945, Prominent Arabs in Germany, NARA, RG 319 IRR Rekowski, Carl Berthold, XA 20393; Document XX-8002, NARA, RG 263, E ZZ-18, B 58, Haj Amin al-Husseini Name File, vol. I, part 1. The source on Husseini's villa is Account in German by Mrs. el-Naggar [June 1946], NARA, RG 319, IRR Naggar, Abdel Halim el, D 052707.

13 Beisner's story is presented below.

14 Herf, *Nazi Propaganda*, 200.

15 Account in German by Mrs. el-Naggar [June 1946], NARA, RG 319, IRR Naggar, Abdel Haleim el, D 052707. El-Naggar went back to working for the Propaganda Ministry and the Foreign Office. Near the end of the war he moved to Prague. He beat his wife (again) badly after she failed to destroy all the documents in his Berlin apartment that connected him with the Nazi regime.

16 Document XX-8830, old pouch, November 1-26,1944, NARA, RG 263, E ZZ-18, B 58, Haj Amin al-Husseini Name File, v. 1, f. 1.

17 Wash X-2-Int-49 Balkan Censorship folder 1, March 15, 1944, and Document XX-8002, NARA, RG 263, E ZZ-18, B 58, Haj Amin al-Husseini Name Fil, v. 1, f. 1.

18 NARA, RG 319, IRR Grand Mufti, Agreement with German Reich, MSN 53144.

19 Report BX-181 from Bern, May 17, 1945, NARA, RG 263, E ZZ-18, B 58, Haj Amin al-Husseini Name File, v. 1, f. 1. Zvi Elpeleg, *The Grand Mufti, Haj Amin al-Hussaini, Founder of the Palestinian National Movement* (London: Frank Cass, 1993), pp. 76–77, Husseini's fear of being prosecuted at Nuremberg increased when he learned that Hermann Krumey gave written evidence in Switzerland that Husseini was involved in encouraging the Nazi destruction of the Jews.

20 OSS R &A document 1090, May 26, 1945, copy in NARA, RG 263, E ZZ-18, B 58, Haj Amin al-Husseini Name File, v. 1, f. 1.

21 Gensicke, *Der Mufti von Jerusalem und die Nationalsozialisten*, 148. Burrell to Blum, March 7, 1946, NARA, RG 263, E ZZ-18, B 58, Haj Amin al-Husseini Name File, v. 1, f. 1.

22 Floyd A. Spencer, Asst. Military Attaché, Cairo Report, Background of Plan to Return … Husseini to Middle East, June 21, 1946, NARA, RG 165, Army G-2 3161.0503, MIS 279421.

23 Floyd A. Spencer, Asst. Military Attaché, Cairo Report, Background of Plan to Return … Husseini to Middle East, June 21, 1946, NARA, RG 165, Army G-2 3161.0503, MIS 279421.

24 The Escape of the Grand Mufti of Jerusalem, August 2, 1946, NARA, RG 263, Grumbach Series 12, Finished Reports. We are grateful to Randy Herrschaft for this reference.

25 Palestine: Views of Mufti: Desire for British Neutrality. Remarks of the Mufti to an experienced Arab source, May 14, 1947, and Reuters article of March 4, 1961, NARA, RG 263, E ZZ-18, B 58, Haj Amin al-Husseini Name File, v. 1, f. 1 and v. 2, f. 1.

26 Bern Report B-2461, April 12, 1945, copy in NARA, RG 263, E ZZ-18, B 10, Friedrich Beissner Name File. The CIA file name is based on a confusion about his first name Wilhelm and middle name Friedrich. It also misspells Beisner, something that Nazi officials themselves often did. We have followed the CIA's spelling and name errors in footnotes using the CIA file.

27 SS Personnel Main Office to Beissner [sic], September 28, 1939, copy in NARA, RG 263, E ZZ-18, B 10, Friedrich Beissner Name File.

28 Mallmann and Cüppers, *Nazi Palestine*, 81. See also Ivo Goldstein and Slavko Goldstein, *Holokaust u Zagrebu* (Zagreb: Novi Liber, 2001), 266, 583, 584.

29 Gottlob Berger to Himmler, April 12, 1941, NARA, RG 242, microcopy T-175, reel 123, frame 2648997.

30 Verleihung eines Kroatischen Ordens, October 16, 1943, NARA, RG 242, microcopy A-3343, SS Officer Files, reel 54.

31 Mallmann and Cüppers, *Nazi Palestine*, 118.

32 Traces, November 10, 1949 and Nachrichtenagent Willi Beissner, May 9, 1950, both in NARA, RG 263, E ZZ-18, B 10, Friedrich Beissner Name File. The information in the second document stemmed from the Gehlen Organization.

33 French North Africa—Tunis—German Intelligence Service During Occupation, November 15, 1944; Saint London to Saint Washington, July 17, 1944; NARA, RG 263, E ZZ-18, B 10, Friedrich Beissner Name File.

34 Nachrichtenagent Willi Beissner, May 9, 1950, both in NARA, RG 263, E ZZ-18, B 10, Friedrich Beissner Name File.

35 Chief of Station Vienna to Chief of Station Karlsruhe, December 8, 1950, and Chief of Station Karlsruhe to Chief of Station Vienna, December 29, 1950, and January 8, 1951, NARA, RG 263, E ZZ-18, B 10, Friedrich Beissner Name File.

36 Beissner, Willi, Egypt, April 4, 1952, and CS-7845, April 30, 1953, NARA, RG 263, E ZZ-18, B 10, Friedrich Beissner Name File.

37 Pull 6790, IN 48795, February 19, 1957, NARA, RG 263, E ZZ-18, B 10, Friedrich Beissner Name File.

38 From NEA-2, Hajj Amin al-Husayni, December 10, 1952, NARA, RG 263, E ZZ-18, B 60, Haj Amin al-Husseini Name File, v. 5, f. 2.

39 Report CS-7845, April 30, 1953, NARA, RG 263, E ZZ-18, B 10, Friedrich Beissner Name File.

40 NECA-1153, To Chief NEA, November 27, 1953, NARA, RG 263, E ZZ-18, B 10, Friedrich Beissner Name File.

41 Chief of Base, Munich to Chief of Station, Germany, February 17, 1958, NARA, RG 263, E ZZ-18, B 10, Friedrich Beissner Name File.

42 D-819 Report, 66th CIC Group, and Andrew N. Havre to Commanding Officer, Region IV, 66th CIC Group, November 23, 1954; and Warren S. Leroy to Assistant Chief of Staff G-2, November 23, 1954, NARA, RG 319, IRR Beisner, Wilhelm XE 00819.

43 IN-39568, March 6, 1958, DAMA, March 7, 1958, and 1961 chart of Beisner's connections, NARA, RG 263, E ZZ-18, B 10, Friedrich Beissner Name File.

44 Central Registry, 66th CIC Group, June 30, 1959, NARA, RG 319, IRR Deumling, Joachim, XE 017494.

45 JX 5911, undated, and JX-6019, July 7, 1954, NARA, RG 263, E ZZ-18, B 23, Joachim Deumling Name File.

46 Mallmann and Cüppers *Nazi Palestine*, p. 205.

47 IN-48099, to Director Cairo, March 25, 1958, and OUT-72412, from Director, March 26 [?] 1958, NARA, RG 263, E ZZ-18, B 10, Friedrich Beissner Name File.

48 See Christopher R. Browning, *The Final Solution and the German Foreign Office* (New York: Holmes and Meier, 1978), pp. 191–93.

49 EGF-2517, November 12, 1957, NARA, RG 319, IRR Rademacher, Franz, XE 304625.

50 Attachment to Hook Dispatch 1069, February 2, 1959, Willi Beissner, and EGMA 40944, March 9, 1959, NARA, RG 263, E ZZ-18, B 10, Friedrich Beissner Name File.

51 Mallmann and Cüppers, *Nazi Palestine*, p. 205. Chief, Munich Liaison Base to Chief, EE, October 20, 1960, NARA, RG 263, E ZZ-18, B 10, Friedrich Beissner Name File.

52 EGMA-52899, January 10, 1961, NARA, RG 263, E ZZ-18, B 10, Friedrich Beissner Name File.

53 EGOA-14075, Chief of Station Germany to Chief, EE, April 3, 1961, NARA, RG 263, E ZZ-18, B 10, Friedrich Beissner Name File. CIA ultimately concluded that the ambiguous first letter was an R. Alois Brunner used both pseudonyms and others besides.

54 EGMA-54517, Chief, Munich Operations Group to Chief, EE, April 20, 1961; and EGOA-14451, Chief of Station, Germany to Chief EE, May 12, 1961, NARA, RG 263, E ZZ-18, B 10, Friedrich Beissner Name File.

55 Munich to Director, April 25, 1961, NARA, RG 263, E ZZ-18, B 19, Alois Brunner Name File.

56 Chief, Munich Operations Group to Chief, NE, May 10, 1961, NARA, RG 263, E ZZ-18, B 19, Alois Brunner Name File.

57 EGMA-58837, Chief Munich Liaison Base to Chief EE, May 21, 1962, NARA, RG 263, E ZZ-18, B 103, Franz Rademacher Name File.

58 Browning, *The Final Solution and the German Foreign Office*, pp. 196–201.

59 See Breitman, et. al., *U.S. Intelligence and the Nazis*, pp. 160–64. The [Israeli] assassination attempt is mentioned in EGMA-58837, Chief Munich Liaison Base to Chief EE, May 21, 1962, NARA, RG 263, E ZZ-18, B 103, Franz Rademacher Name File.

Rudolf Mildner, SIPO and SD in Denmark, was charged by Gruppenfuhrer Muller to detain or arrest Danish physicist Niels Bohr. Bohr, however, was able to escape first to Sweden and then to Britain and did not become part of Germany's efforts to build atomic weapons. Mildner himself was captured and held initially at Dachau and later at Nuremberg. He was about to be extradited to Poland for war crimes, when he escaped and later resurfaced in Argentina. *RG 319, Records of the Army Staff.*

CHAPTER THREE

New Materials on Former Gestapo Officers

Gestapo officers, who also held ranks in the SS, were in the U.S. Army Counterintelligence Corps's automatic arrest category after the war. Initially, the CIC viewed them as security threats because they could arrange continued clandestine resistance against the occupation. Later, CIC used former Gestapo officers to garner useful intelligence for the postwar period on everything from German right-wing movements to underground communist organizations. Intelligence officers often overlooked the significant role Gestapo officers played in the murder of Jews, POWs, and the political enemies of the Nazis.

More than 25 years ago Allan A. Ryan, author of the 1983 official U.S. Government study of the Klaus Barbie case, noted that a growing number of Gestapo personnel were released from U.S. captivity in 1946 and 1947 and "their apparent use grew, although to what extent is uncertain."[1] The newly released records provide a much fuller picture regarding the American use of Gestapo officers. The CIC went to some lengths to protect certain persons from justice. The following cases are representative.

Rudolf Mildner's Escape from Justice

Rudolf Mildner was originally arrested as part of a search for Nazi officials who might lead an underground Nazi resistance. On May 21, 1945, the Counter-

Intelligence War Room in London asked Allied forces in the field to learn from captured Reich Security Main Office (RSHA) members what instructions they had been given for continued activity after Germany's defeat. In the weeks ahead the War Room learned that important Gestapo officials had concentrated around Hof near Munich, Salzburg, and Innsbruck in the war's final days.[2] On May 30, 1945, the 80th CIC detachment in the Austrian Alps captured Mildner, a senior Gestapo official. He claimed that he was climbing for recreation and that he had intended to surrender to the Americans.[3] It was the first of many misrepresentations.

A native Austrian with radical rightist sympathies, Mildner received a law degree in 1934. In July of the same year, the illegal Austrian Nazi movement assassinated Chancellor Engelbert Dollfuss. Afterwards, Mildner fled Austria for Munich. Reinhard Heydrich, then head of the Gestapo, hired him to investigate other Austrians who had crossed into Germany to determine who was reliable. Mildner later claimed that Heydrich forced him to remain in the German police, but Heydrich would not have trusted a reluctant officer for such duty. Mildner, in fact, became deputy chief of the Gestapo in Linz, Hitler's hometown, after Germany annexed Austria in March 1938.[4]

U.S. authorities knew that Mildner was a long-standing Gestapo member but never pressed him for details on the Gestapo's crimes against Jews or anyone else. Mildner simply misled them. In discussing his functions late in the war as acting chief of Vienna's Security Police, he mentioned that he left untouched Vienna's remnant of 15,000 Jews.[5] He hardly deserved credit. Nazi authorities never decided what to do with Jews in mixed marriages in Germany owing to "Aryan" partners' reactions, which included a major protest in Berlin in February 1943.[6] But U.S. Army Capt. Andrew R. Pickens found Mildner cooperative and possessing a good memory. The War Room told the CIC that "it is not thought that his information of Amt IV [Gestapo] is likely to be of outstanding interest as it seems probably that his service at the RSHA was merely marking time."[7]

Mildner left out large parts of his career. As head of the Jewish section of the Vienna Gestapo from 1941–43, he signed orders confiscating the property of some 10,000 Viennese Jews deported to Auschwitz.[8] As Gestapo chief in Katowice in East Upper Silesia from 1941 to 1943, he was responsible for the execution of hundreds, if not thousands, of suspected Polish resisters. Mildner gave them one-minute "trials" in the infamous Block 11 of Auschwitz concentration camp that resulted in shooting or hanging. He came to Auschwitz frequently for this purpose.[9]

Mildner also failed to mention that he had been commander of the Security Police and SD in Denmark in the fall of 1943 when Hitler and Himmler ordered Denmark's 8,000 Jews arrested and deported to Auschwitz. Denmark's Jews escaped this fate owing to the courageous German naval attaché, Georg Duckwitz, who leaked Berlin's intentions to Danish officials, leading to a mass escape to Sweden. Finally, Mildner said nothing about his serving as deputy chief of the RSHA office over Adolf Eichmann in the spring of 1944 when Eichmann and his task force went to Hungary to arrange the deportation of hundreds of thousands of Hungarian Jews to Auschwitz.

Bits of the truth slowly emerged from Mildner's associates, some of them were also captured and interrogated. Karl Ebner, a former deputy, told the British that Mildner approved the execution of a British agent dropped by parachute near Vienna in mid-1944.[10] Franz Joseph Huber, Mildner's one-time superior as Security Police Inspector for the Vienna region, admitted visiting Dachau in 1936, Sachsenhausen in 1936, and Mauthausen in 1939. But, he said, he had never seen any cruelty there, that the laws of humanity were always his highest rule of conduct, and that he never believed in blind obedience or foolhardy resistance.[11] The main Allied interest in Huber centered on the whereabouts of Gestapo Chief Heinrich Müller.[12] The Allies were still trying to determine whether Müller had died in the last days of the war.[13]

Because Mildner mentioned a mid-April 1945 order from Heinrich Himmler through RSHA chief Ernst Kaltenbrunner to prepare for postwar underground resistance, he was a potentially useful witness against Kaltenbrunner and the SS generally at the Trial of the Major War Criminals in Nuremberg. On October 1 the CIC turned him over to the U.S. Chief of Counsel for War Crimes. It recommended his internment after he had served his purpose at Nuremberg, presumably because his SS rank made him liable to automatic arrest. But Army Intelligence (G-2) Headquarters, which had not cleared his transfer to Nuremberg, complained to CIC that they wanted additional access. The Judge Advocate General's office agreed to notify G-2 when Mildner was finished at Nuremberg.[14]

While Mildner was in Nuremberg, the Military Intelligence Service Center issued an interim report about him. It deserves attention mostly for its conclusions and final comments about Mildner's last weeks in Vienna. The analysts found that Mildner had not done anything to set up an underground movement that might cause postwar problems. They considered his memory excellent, thought he had spoken freely, and considered him reliable. The short final interrogation report on Mildner, dated January 11, 1946, broke no new ground, calling him reliable and very cooperative. The Army sent a copy of this report to the FBI.[15]

In the meantime, war crimes investigators at Nuremberg examined Mildner's career more carefully. Former subordinates from Katowice testified that he had ordered the execution of 500–600 Poles at Auschwitz. When Mildner learned about this evidence in late January 1946, he broke down, refused to eat, and showed signs of depression. When examined by American psychiatrist Leon Goldensohn, he rationalized: "Suppose you Americans were in Germany fighting Russia, and some Germans sabotaged you, or shot your soldiers, or stole. You'd hang them. And rightly so. So to preserve order and prevent sabotage, the Germans in Poland and Silesia had to do that too."[16]

A Danish lawyer also interviewed Mildner at Nuremberg about his time in Denmark. Mildner accentuated the positive, claiming that Gestapo Chief Müller ordered him to arrest the Nobel Prize–winning atomic physicist Niels Bohr. In the fall of 1943 Bohr was in jeopardy partly because he was half-Jewish. But Berlin also recognized his scientific importance, and the Gestapo in Denmark received an order from Berlin to arrest him specifically. A German woman working for the Gestapo who had seen the order tipped off Mrs. Bohr's brother-in-law. The Bohrs fled across the Kattegat to Sweden shortly before the mass flight of Danish Jews there.[17] Mildner mentioned the arrest order, but said that he had refused to arrest Bohr. In Mildner's retelling, this allowed Bohr's escape. A Danish newspaper published this far-fetched account on March 21.[18]

Ironically the OSS learned back in 1944 how substantial Mildner's role in Denmark actually was. A Danish policeman who went to Sweden compiled a detailed report on the German police in Denmark, which reached the OSS in April 1944. The report discounted the role of Higher SS and Police Leader Günter Pancke, nominally the top police executive there, because he was frequently absent. Mildner, said the report, was the dominant police official. Mildner's deputy Dr. Hoffmann supervised a concentration camp at Horseröd.[19] But by October 1945 the OSS was dissolved, and the information never reached the Army or War Crimes officials in Europe. (It was not declassified until 2000.)

In April 1946 Nuremberg prosecutors interrogated Mildner about Kaltenbrunner. As before, Mildner incriminated Kaltenbrunner for his efforts to organize last ditch resistance. In mid-April 1945 Kaltenbrunner had ordered him and others to set up a network of SD and Gestapo agents and saboteurs to operate behind enemy lines at war's end.[20] Around the same time, former Auschwitz Commandant Rudolf Höss also testified at Nuremberg. Höss noted that he had showed Mildner the entire camp including the gas chambers and crematoria. Mildner was quite interested, Höss said, because he was deporting Jews from Katowice to Auschwitz.[21] It was a most damning account.

In April 1946 the British requested Mildner's extradition, probably because of the case of the executed British agent. CIC said it had no further interest in him and did not object to extradition. A cryptic handwritten note on the memo indicated that he was placed in Rogues Galley on May 4.[22] In June Danish intelligence wanted to pose more questions to Mildner about the case of Niels Bohr. How much did Nazi authorities know about Bohr, and why didn't Mildner arrest him? The Danes sent a list of questions for American authorities to put to Mildner. But, according to CIC records, on August 11, 1946, Mildner escaped from Civilian Internment Camp #409 in Nuremberg. By the time Poland also requested his extradition in December, his file indicates that his location was unknown.[23]

While in U.S. custody, Mildner described every branch and stem of Vienna's Gestapo organization. A broad sample of other captured Vienna policemen also gave details to the Military Intelligence Research Service in Austria about their organization and their fellow officers. In November 1946 the Military Intelligence Service put out a 142-page report on the Gestapo in Vienna. Army Intelligence in Austria received 11 copies; the 430th CIC detachment in Austria received 19 copies; the Office of U.S. Chief of Counsel (for War Crimes) received a single copy. Tracking and punishing war criminals were not high among the Army's priorities in late 1946.[24]

One must infer why the U.S. Army put in such effort to reconstruct Gestapo organizational charts. Occupying parts of Germany and Austria, U.S. forces needed to keep order, and any diehard Nazi police forces represented a threat. On the other hand, more pragmatic German policemen who had dealt with security issues such as Communist espionage or subversion might have useful skills and detailed knowledge. The Army initially seemed to consider Mildner one of the useful officials. Whether the CIC's lenient treatment of Mildner contributed in some way to his ability to escape will remain unknown unless more information surfaces. There is one suggestive source: Nuremberg psychiatrist Leon Goldensohn believed Mildner remained in American custody until 1949.[25] It is possible that in return for his services, U.S. forces protected Mildner against extradition. In 1949, like a number of other Nazi war criminals, Mildner went to Argentina. He later crossed paths there with his former colleague Adolf Eichmann.[26]

The Gestapo and the Struggle Against Communism:
The Gestapo in Baden

In the spring of 1947 a CIC agent named Robert S. Taylor from CIC Region IV (Munich) recruited Klaus Barbie, the one-time Gestapo Chief of Lyon (1942–44). Barbie helped run a counterintelligence net named "Büro Petersen" which monitored French intelligence. In 1948 Barbie helped the CIC locate former Gestapo informants. In 1949–50, he penetrated German Communist Party (KPD) activities in CIC Region XII (Augsburg). Unaware of Barbie's initial hiring in 1947, CIC headquarters was ambivalent about retaining him. Regardless, he continued to work for the CIC in return for protection against French war crimes charges. The story of his escape to South America with the help of the CIC, after French authorities began to make inquiries as to his whereabouts in 1951, is well known.[27]

The latest batch of CIC records has more information about the process of hiring Gestapo officials. Allan Ryan quotes a CIC headquarters June 7, 1949, directive from Maj. Earl Browning titled "Brief and Policy for the Interrogation and Exploitation of Gestapo Personnel." It called for the reinterrogation of Gestapo specialists regarding KPD methods and possible agents that could be used within the KPD itself. But the directive had limits. "It is the policy of this Headquarters," Browning wrote, "to discourage the use of Gestapo personnel as further sources of this organization except in unusual circumstances."[28] Either this directive was frequently disregarded, or there were a lot of unusual circumstances.

Approximately 1,200 newly released files relate to the penetration of German Communist activities and specifically to "Project Happiness," the CIC's codename for counterintelligence operations against the KPD. A smaller number of files relate specifically to the location of and use of Gestapo personnel as agents and informants in the different CIC regions. The example of the Baden region in West Germany suggests that the CIC's relationship with Gestapo officers depended partly on the individuals involved. Some former Gestapo officers were more willing to cooperate than others.

In August 1949 CIC Headquarters requested organizational charts of the Gestapo in Baden (CIC Region II) in order to exploit former Gestapo Communist experts there.[29] In 1945 CIC had undertaken studies based on interrogations of arrested Gestapo members, but these studies were organizational in nature and were handicapped by the fact that in many cities, Heidelberg for instance, Gestapo officers received orders to burn their records.[30] Regional CIC officers now reconstructed Gestapo personnel lists for the major cities including Mannheim, Heidelberg, and Karlsruhe. They included potential Communist experts from the Gestapo, together with up-to-date addresses and notes on Gestapo personnel who might have fled south to the French occupation zone.

Some Gestapo personnel in northern Baden had already been sentenced for war crimes. Hermann Boschert of the Karlsruhe Gestapo was serving a life sentence (subsequently shortened) for his role in the murder of an escaped British POW even though, in the CIC's assessment, he "may be termed an expert on communism."[31] Eugen Feucht of the Heidelberg Gestapo "was the most active man in the political field," according to former Gestapo co-workers. In 1949 he was serving a three-year prison term for his wartime activities. Regardless, special agent Fred C. Hicks noted that "[I] will make an attempt to contact Feucht in the very near future."[32]

Others refused to talk for fear of self-incrimination. "A burned child avoids fire," said Hermann Kraut, the former head of the Baden Gestapo's Referat N (which managed and registered informants), who worked in 1950 as a watchmaker, "and for that reason I won't do any more political work." Kraut told the CIC that he "had been contacted numerous times by an American civilian organization … but that he refused to work for that organization, regardless of how much they would pay him."[33] Johann Oettinger had been in charge of the Gestapo in Heidelberg but claimed to have no contact with any of his office's former informants. Special Agent Hicks wrote that, "Oettinger does not want to give any information to this office."[34]

The efforts of Special Agent Ralph Kahn in Mannheim, well documented in the new records, suggest expanded use of former Gestapo personnel to penetrate the KPD. In 1949 Kahn contacted every former Gestapo officer of possible value in Mannheim. He had mixed success. Fritz Michel was, according to former colleagues, "the most capable man the local Gestapo had in the leftist political field after 1933." At first, Michel was unwilling to help owing to "the harsh treatment he allegedly received during his internment in Ludwigsburg…." Kahn noted that, "he was very cold toward this agent when the first contacts were made." Kahn persevered. "Only after many visits," Kahn reported on December 19, 1949, "did [Michel] slowly warm up and begin to talk."

"You think that we had the Mannheim KPD penetrated," Michel told Kahn in mid-December, "but that is not the case. We had no penetration in Mannheim at any time from 1933 to 1945." "We had some lucky breaks in Mannheim," Michel continued, "and were able to get some good cases, but we did not get them through any 'Spitzels' [police spies] whom we had placed within the party." Michel said that the Mannheim Gestapo depended on routine denunciations. "The Gestapo," he said, "had at times some voluntary informants who did not like some person, and from these leads, we could occasionally get a fairly good case." The Gestapo arrested the occasional KPD functionary and then "worked on him" until he gave up more names of active KPD members. This, Michel said, was how the Mannheim Gestapo destroyed the communist resistance circle under Georg Lechleiter in 1942, a case that led to 31 arrests and 19 executions including that of Lechleiter himself.[35] Michel told Kahn that he knew many KPD functionaries in the Mannheim area, but was "allegedly not able to give any names as to who could be recruited as informants."[36]

Kahn repeatedly contacted Adolf Gerst, the former head of the Mannheim Gestapo, who was subject to murder charges. Gerst later received a seven-year sentence for aggressive interrogations that ended in death.[37] Gerst claimed little contact with former informants because, as he said, "his agents usually contacted the informants." Kahn reported that he "made a strenuous effort" to obtain employment for Gerst's son, also named Adolf, who had just been released from prison by the French for his role in the Gestapo in Saarbrücken. Kahn reported that "this did not persuade Gerst to give information…."[38]

In August 1949 the CIC learned that Alois Bischoff, "an expert on communism," had been from late 1943 to 1945 the head of Mannheim's Referat-N and "was considered the key, and most capable man of this Referat." Kahn located him after his denazification hearings. Bischoff was unemployed and still a believer in National Socialism—he had joined the Party in 1927.[39] Bischoff refused to incriminate himself or give information on right-wing groups "because of his former party activities and his belief in that party." But he was pleased to provide information on the political left. "An offer to pay [Bischoff] for his time spent in talking … about former informants or contacts, was emphatically refused…." Bischoff thus revealed for free that Referat N had numerous carded informants within illegal party organizations, including Gerhard Jakobshagen, an SPD member of the former Baden State Parliament, who had contacts in the KPD and provided information of illegal SPD activity. He also noted, contrary to Michel's assertion, that the Gestapo had an informant who helped with the Lechleiter case. Kahn followed these leads further and maintained the relationship with Bischoff.[40]

The Cases of Eugen Fischer and Anton Mahler

The cases of Eugen Fischer and Anton Mahler, two senior Gestapo officers in Munich and Augsburg, demonstrate similarities to the Barbie case. Historians have known since the 1980s that the CIC had relationships with them. But their CIC files provide many new details.[41]

Both men were career policemen before 1933. Fischer joined the Bavarian police in Munich in 1924 and had engaged in intelligence and political work. He joined the Nazi Party in 1934 and served in the Munich Gestapo from 1936 forward.[42] Mahler joined the Nazi Party (NSDAP) in 1933 and served in the Augsburg Gestapo from 1938 to 1941. From December 1941 to February 1945, he was part of the Munich Gestapo then transferred back to Augsburg until the end of the war.[43] During the war they served together in Gestapo section IV A, where they investigated high treason cases by the illegal KPD.

Mahler is of interest for two other reasons. He was the chief interrogator of Hans Scholl, a leading member of the White Rose, a student organization in Munich that decried German apathy and called for Hitler's overthrow through the secret distribution of leaflets. Hans and his sister Sophie Scholl were convicted of high treason and beheaded in February 1943. From May to November 1941, Mahler also served in Einsatzgruppe B in occupied Belarus, which participated in the killings of more than 45,000 people, most of them Jews, by mid-November 1941.[44] It is not clear what Mahler did in Belarus. Einsatzgruppe B began its campaign with 665 members.[45] This admission on his own U.S. Military Government questionnaire in 1947 was ignored or overlooked by U.S. and West German authorities, and Mahler never mentioned it subsequently.

In the automatic arrest category, both men were apprehended shortly after the war.[46] Fischer was originally placed in the War Crimes enclosure in Dachau, but the authorities lacked evidence of his crimes. He was moved to Moosberg labor enclosure pending denazification proceedings.

In August 1947 CIC Region IV (Munich) discovered that Fischer had been in Gestapo Office IV A 2 (Counter-Sabotage). "It is assumed," noted Lt. Col. L. M. de Riemer, the commanding officer of the 970th CIC Detachment on August 26, 1947, "that many old KPD members who were known to [Fischer] are presently active in important positions," and "that [Fischer] could be helpful in supplying many details." "It is highly urgent" he added, "that CIC Region IV have access to the information [Fischer] can supply before he meets the Denazification Board. This information cannot be solicited while [Fischer] is confined in the Internment Center."[47] The U.S. Military Government (OMGUS) had to approve his release. Region IV asked that Fischer receive a one-month furlough. OMGUS's Public Safety Branch agreed to release Fischer for one month, on the condition that any help for the CIC not affect his pending denazification hearing.[48] Fischer went through denazification but emerged unscathed.[49]

After Fischer's furlough became indefinite in January 1948, the CIC incorporated him into Project Happiness. He worked in the Augsburg and Munich regions, first as part of Barbie's Petersen net, and then as an independent source for various CIC special agents. By all accounts he was valuable. An experienced police officer, he had numerous contacts in city and state police in Bavaria, and as a former Gestapo officer, he maintained contact with former Gestapo sources. He thus developed extensive contacts and penetrated city and state police offices, various civil agencies, private concerns, and even right-wing political groups in order to investigate KPD penetration of these organizations. In 1949 he was responsible for written reports on KPD activities in the MAN (Maschinenfabrik Augsburg Nürnberg) factory in Augsburg, the KPD penetration of the Augsburg city police, as well as reports on the Soviet zone.[50]

At the same time Fischer was a security hazard. Maj. Henry V. Ida of CIC Region XII (Augsburg) pointed to the "undesirability of hiring former Gestapo agents as full time "X" type informants." Ignoring the basics of compartmentalization, the CIC allowed Fischer to be handled by three separate agents, including Special

Agent Erhard Dabringhaus, who handled Barbie as of June 1948 and had a reputation for lax security. Fischer became familiar with general CIC practices in the Augsburg and Munich regions and with the identities of numerous older and newer sources used by more than one CIC Regional office. Because of Fischer's extensive knowledge of CIC sources and methods, Ida worried that "dropping [Fischer] at this time may do more harm than good."

Instead, Ida began to shift Fischer's activities away from Project Happiness to "projects of less sensitivity and importance," such as the "investigation of the activities of former Gestapo, SS and NSDAP officials." Region XII also tried to learn Fischer's own sub-sources as well as what Fischer knew of CIC sources and methods. This task was difficult owing to Fischer's "extreme reluctance to submit sufficient information regarding his sub-sources…. Overly precipitous action in this respect will make [Fischer] aware that he is being 'debriefed.'"[51]

Mahler's case was similar to Fischer's. Released from U.S. detention in September 1948, Mahler faced denazification in Augsburg almost immediately.[52] He intended to protect himself in the proceeding by naming Max Lappler, a local KPD functionary, as a wartime Gestapo informant. Lappler was now working as an informant for Fischer. To protect Mahler and his source within the KPD, Fischer wrote the U.S. authorities in hopes of postponing Mahler's denazification hearing, adding that, "the KPD had a definite political interest in eliminating former Gestapo officials who were specialists in Communist questions, through the Spruchkammer [Denazification Courts]."[53] Mahler's hearing labeled him an "Activist" (i.e., not a "Major Offender"). Still, he immediately appealed the finding with the argument that the hearing was politically inspired by the local KPD. The Spruchkammer decision was nullified on September 24, 1949, though the circumstances are unclear.[54] Mahler's restraint in mentioning old Gestapo sources made him suitable for intelligence work.[55] His resumé, submitted to the CIC, mentioned his work against Communists in the Gestapo and omitted his service in Einsatzgruppe B.

CIC Region XII used Mahler as an informant beginning in February 1949. By May, he was a full-time employee at Region XII, performing secretarial duties and holding daily discussions with Special Agent Herbert Bechtold about the KPD and its methods. At the same time, Mahler worked for Fischer. He received 300 marks per month plus cigarettes, coffee, soap, and razor blades. It was an improvement over his first postwar job as a construction laborer.[56]

The KPD was not finished with Fischer and Mahler. In November 1949, members of the KPD in Munich aided by the Union of Nazi Persecutees (VVN)—an organization with communist connections—brought criminal complaints against each to the Bavarian State Court in Munich. Based on information from their sources within the KPD, Fischer and Mahler argued to their U.S. handlers that the criminal complaints were politics by other means—an effort by the KPD to eliminate their former Gestapo adversaries through criminal trials when denazification had not done the job. The KPD, according to Fischer's sources, also understood that this case would expose the U.S. agencies that were protecting Fischer and Mahler, while eliminating the two former Gestapo anti-Communist operatives. The VVN, said Fischer, prepared the case by rounding up additional witnesses through advertisements, even if the ads could provide nothing but hearsay from family members of alleged victims. The VVN hoped that the sheer bulk of witnesses, together with an intimidating crowd in the courtroom, would result in convictions. According to Fischer and Mahler, the KPD even tried to recruit their former Security Police colleagues as prosecution witnesses, offering to vouch for them during their own denazification hearings should they testify against Fischer and Mahler.

CIC Region IV told CIC headquarters that Fischer and Mahler should be protected from politically inspired criminal proceedings:

> ….either of them may have been forced [in the Gestapo] to use methods of interrogation which are not condoned as regular practice, but, in times of emergency and with pressure from superiors exerted, these methods can by no means be classified as atrocities…. every effort should be made to prevent a trial of these men on the present basis, not so much because a miscarriage of justice should be prevented, but because the interests of this agency and perhaps to a great extent the entire United States occupation forces could be protected…. As indicated by a number of events, the KPD had learned of Fischer's usage by Region IV and by this Headquarters some time ago. The possibility exists that a plan was arranged then, whereby perhaps two flies could be killed with one stroke, the elimination of Fischer and the discovery of the amount of penetration effected by him within the KPD.[57]

The response by CIC headquarters is not located in CIC files on Fischer or Mahler, but a later comment by Col. David Erskine, the CIC 66th

Detachment's commanding officer, suggests that senior CIC officers took a different tack. As Erskine explained later to his superiors at OMGUS,

> The [Fischer] net was ... neutralized and eventually disbanded when it became unwieldy and began to exhibit a lack of requisite security. Meanwhile, Fischer became a definite security problem for this organization. It was felt that he would require an extensive 'debriefing' period before he could be safely dropped by this organization. The debriefing process was well underway at the time the Subject was brought to trial and convicted. The conviction, in actuality, gave this organization a 'stated' reason to more speedily terminate its relationship with Subject.[58]

In short, the CIC did not protect Fischer and Mahler. It allowed the trial to go forward as a way to neutralize Fischer, perhaps in the expectation that neither man would reveal his sources to the German authorities.

Fischer and Mahler stood trial in Bavarian State Court in Munich from December 19–22, 1949, for their excesses during their Gestapo service. Mahler's service in Einsatzgruppe B never came up in this trial. There were originally 14 complaints against Fischer and 12 against Mahler, most centering on beatings of Communists during interrogations. For many of the accusers, the trial was political from the start. "Now we'll at least have two of this gang," said one witness.[59] Several witnesses out of more than 40 that were called tempered their testimonies once warned of the penalty for perjury. Other witness statements were based on hearsay. Yet Fischer was still found guilty of beating prisoners and forcing confessions in six cases (two confessions led to executions). Mahler was found guilty of three beatings and one confession forced through threats.

Their sentences were relatively mild. Both Gestapo functionaries broke German laws governing police interrogations that were still technically valid under the Nazis. But the court gave allowance for the fact that Fischer and Mahler, as police officers, were trying to uncover cases of high treason in wartime. Fischer received a five-year prison sentence and Mahler a sentence of four years, but each sentence was reduced by 18 months, owing to time already served in Allied enclosures.[60]

The CIC was philosophical. Though some evidence was unreliable and perhaps even perjured, there was also little doubt that the defendants "did strike and mistreat some prisoners." "Considering the pressure on the judge [and] the unruly mob of KPD people in the courtroom," noted Special Agent Siegfried Clemens, the verdicts were as favorable to the former Gestapo officers as could be expected.[61] And Fischer revealed no CIC sources during the trial. "Whether the results of the trial will affect the prestige of CIC in the Munich-Augsburg area remains to be seen," reported Maj. George Riggin, "but it is doubted at the present time…. [To] date there have been no indications that any KPD sources have been or will be compromised. It is not anticipated that Fischer will reveal any sources known to him." In February 1950 the CIC officially dropped him.[62]

Both men fled Munich before the sentencing session and lived in hiding thereafter.[63] West German state authorities asked the U.S. High Commission under John McCloy to locate them. Erskine from the 66th Detachment Headquarters noted as late as October 1950 that he had no objection. Fischer had been dropped. Yet Erskine also noted in October that the CIC had "no information concerning the present whereabouts of these two men."[64] Skeptical West German police authorities placed the CIC Region IV Headquarters in Augsburg under surveillance on the assumption that both men were secretly employed there.[65]

While a sampling of relevant files does not establish Fischer's whereabouts, it also reveals that Mahler went back to work for the CIC just days after his disappearance. A handwritten directive from Special Agent Eugene Kolb, who was then still handling Barbie, warned other agents "to be extremely careful with F 9 M [Mahler]. Contacts should if possible either be discontinued or made outside of Augsburg … any indication of police surveillance is to be brought to my attention immediately."[66]

In July 1950, Special Agent Herbert Bechtold reported that, in keeping with the June 7, 1949, directive from Browning, "former Gestapo agents of primary importance are now being re-contacted for a total exploitation of all phases of their experience not previously covered in the more cursory interrogation. This phase of the investigation pertains primarily to leads and cases once handled by these agents…." In Mahler's case, this involved his 1943 investigation of the White Rose. To Mahler, it was an unfinished case because, even though the White Rose leaders were arrested, tried, and in some cases executed, there were loose ends. The White Rose case also gave Mahler an additional chance to re-establish his anti-communist bona fides with the United States.

Mahler's July 14, 1950, report on "Sedition Activities of the Scholl Twins" is of interest to scholars of the White Rose insofar as the 17-page report includes Gestapo efforts to stop the distribution of anti-Hitler leaflets before the arrest of Hans and Sophie Scholl in February 1943. But it also paints Hans Scholl, whom Mahler interrogated, as a Communist. Scholl came, Mahler said, from a "Marxistic (sic) oriented family, which nevertheless spread a cloak of religious piety over its existence." White Rose leaflets, in Mahler's retelling, "were atheistic and cultural Bolshevistic propaganda…." Under interrogation, Hans Scholl argued "that communism had been a decided improvement over the Czarist dynasty" and that "an alliance between the Soviet Union and Germany could only be advantageous to both nations." Mahler further emphasized that White Rose member Falk Harnack was the brother of Arvid Harnack, a leader in the Soviet spy ring in Germany known as the Red Orchestra, and that the Gestapo had never been able to investigate the possible connections between the two organizations. In reality, there was nothing communistic about any of the White Rose leaflets. But the connection impressed Special Agent Bechtold. He recommended "more active exploitation" of Mahler.

While in hiding, Mahler had his attorney appeal his criminal conviction. The Superior State Court in Munich rejected Mahler's appeal on December 21, 1951. Mahler immediately worried for his safety. He tried to blackmail Max Lappler, a KPD member, with exposure as a CIC informant if Lappler did not produce the "order" by the East German Communist Party (SED) that Mahler thought prompted the West German KPD to use criminal trials to neutralize former Gestapo figures. Such, Mahler thought, would negate his conviction.[67] He also asked West Germany's neo-Nazi party (the Socialist Reich Party) to help him escape Germany for Argentina and to provide him with financial assistance. He cited his loyalty to the Nazi party as making him worthy of its aid.[68] The Mahler file ends with this request.

ENDNOTES

1   Allan A. Ryan, Jr., *Klaus Barbie and the United States Government: The Report, with Documentary Appendix. To the Attorney General of the United States* (Frederick, MD: University Publications of America, 1983).
2   Tactical Interrogation of Members of the RSHA, May 21, 1945, NARA RG 226, Entry 119A, box 22, folder 621. W.R.C. Fortnightly Report, June 18, 1945, NARA RG 226, Entry 119A, box 25, folder 639. Saint to Saint Washington, Info Saint, Austria, War Room Summary ending July 18, NARA RG 226, Entry 88, box 388, folder 645. These documents were declassified in 2000.

3   Carl F. O'Neal, 80th CIC Detachment, Memorandum for the Officer in Charge, May 31, 1945, NARA, RG 319, IRR Mildner, Dr. Rudolf, D 00880.

4   This biographical sketch is drawn from the May 31 interrogation and partly from Mildner's February 1946 interviews conducted by American psychiatrist Leon Goldensohn. See Robert Gellately, ed., *The Nuremberg Interviews: Conducted by Leon Goldensohn* (New York: Knopf, 2004), pp. 368–71.

5   Interrogation Report No. 47, The Gestapo in Vienna, September 11, 1945, p. 9, IRR Mildner, Dr. Rudolf, D 00880.

6   Nathan Stoltzfus, *Resistance of the Heart: Intermarriage and the Rosenstrasse Protest in Nazi Germany* (New York: Norton, 1996).

7   Preliminary Interrogation No. 59, September 5, 1945; Counter-Intelligence War Room, London to USFET, September 11, 1945, NARA, RG 319, IRR Mildner, Dr. Rudolf, D 00880. Interrogation Report No. 47, September 11, 1945, IRR Mildner, Dr. Rudolf, D 00880.

8   Günter Bischoff, Anton Pelinka, Michael Gehler, eds., *Austria in the European Union*, (New Jersey: Transaction Publishers, 2002), p. 293.

9   Debórah Dwork and Robert Jan van Pelt, *Auschwitz: 1270 to the Present* (New York: Norton, 1996), 177–78; Rebecca Wittmann, *Beyond Justice: The Auschwitz Trial* (Cambridge: Harvard University Press, 2005), 104.

10 [British] CSDIC Austria Interrogation of Karl Ebner, August 24–September 2, 1945, NARA, RG 319, IRR Ebner, Dr. Karl, XA 013137. Ebner also showed selective recall. He emphasized that he had quarreled with Mildner and claimed involvement in the July 20, 1944, conspiracy to assassinate Hitler and overthrow the Nazi regime. As a result, Ebner said, he was arrested, imprisoned, and sentenced to death

11 Voluntary statement by Huber, June 25, 1945, NARA, RG 319, IRR Huber, Franz Joseph, D 002609. The Allies did not prosecute Huber. A German denazification tribunal in Nuremberg acquitted him of all responsibility for crimes.

12 Counter-Intelligence War Room, London to USFET Main, December 7, 1945, NARA, RG 319, IRR Huber, Franz Joseph, D 002609.

13 See Chapter 1 above.

14 Heimann to Chief, CIB, G-2, October 11, 1945; G-2 to JA, War Crimes Branch, November 1, 1945, NARA, RG 319, IRR Mildner, Dr. Rudolf, D 00880. The Final Intelligence Report on Mildner, January 11, 1946, however, lists a transfer date of September 24.

15 Interim Intelligence Report/32, December 22, 1945; Final Interrogation Report/70, January 11, 1946, RG 319, NARA, RG 319 IRR Mildner, Dr. Rudolf, D 00880; NARA, RG 65, Classification 65, box 191, File 65-53566.

16 Gellately, ed., *The Nuremberg Interviews*, 368.

17 Thomas Powers, *Heisenberg's War: The Secret History of the German Bomb* (New York: Knopf, 1993), 234–35.

18 Danish General Staff Intelligence Section to Intelligence Bureau, 3 June 1946, NARA, RG 319, IRR Mildner, Dr. Rudolf, D 00880. Mildner mistakenly told Goldenssohn that Bohr had fled later, after the Jews went to Sweden. *The Nuremberg Interviews*, 375–77

19 German Security Police in Denmark, April 20, 1944, NARA, RG 226, Entry 216, box 4, folder 40. This report was rated B-2, which meant OSS considered it reliable. An April 1944 chart showing German authorities in Denmark had SS Colonel Dr. Molder [sic] as commander of the Security Police and SD. NARA, RG 226, Entry 216, box 9, WN 27540-27549.

20 Testimony of Rudolf Mildner taken at Nuremberg, April 25, 1946, NARA, RG 319, IRR Mildner, Dr. Rudolf, D 00880.

21 *TMWC*, v. 11, p. 417.

22 NARA, RG 549, Entry 2223, Box 3.

23 File Memo of February 11, 1948; G-2 Memos of August 24, 1955 and September 9, 1955, NARA RG 319, IRR Mildner, Dr. Rudolf, D 00880.

24 Interrogation Report No. 47, September 11, 1945; Interim Interrogation Report No. 32, December 22, 1945, NARA, RG 319, IRR Mildner, Dr. Rudolf, D 00880. NARA RG 319, IRR Gestapo Vienna, D 152106a.

25 *The Nuremberg Interviews*, 367.

26 Uki Goni, *The Real Odessa: Smuggling the Nazis to Perón's Argentina* (New York: Granta, 2002), p. 308.

27 Ryan, *Klaus Barbie and the United States Government*, passim.

28 Ryan, *Klaus Barbie*, p. 16. For the full directive see Ryan, *Klaus Barbie*, pp. 192–98.

29 Gestapo Communist Experts Progress Report, August 4, 1949, II-419.03, NARA, RG 319, IRR Gestapo Communist Experts, XE 0342X.

30 See for example Memorandum by Special Agent Remy W. Fulscher, June 25, 1945, NARA, RG 319, IRR, Gestapo Aussenstelle Heidelberg, D 035498.

31 Boschert, Heinrich, Card based on Agent Report dated August 4, 1949, NARA, RG 319, IRR, Boschert, Hermann, D 087446. On the case see Priscilla Dale Jones, "Nazi Atrocities Against Allied Airmen: Stalag Luft III and the End of British War Crimes Trials," *The Historical Journal*, v. 41, n. 2 (1998): 543–65.

32 Gestapo Communist Experts Progress Report, August 4, 1949, II-419.03, NARA, RG 319, IRR, XE 00342X.

33 Kraut, Hermann Card, January 16, 1950, NARA, RG 319, IRR, D269249.

34 Gestapo Communist Experts Progress Report, August 4, 1949, II-419.03, NARA, RG 319, IRR Gestapo Communist Experts, XE 00342X.

35 "Georg Lechleiter – Ein Mannheimer Kommunist," *Der Widerstand im deutschen Südwesten 1933–1945*, ed. Michael Bosch and Wolfgang Niess (Stuttgart: Kohlhammer, 1984).

36 Special Agent Ralph Kahn, Mannheim Gestapo, December 19, 1940, NARA, RG 319, IRR Michel, Franz, D 269249.

37 For Gerst's homicide case, see C. F. Rüter and Dick W. de Mildt, eds., *Justiz und NS-Verbrechen: Sammlung deutscher Strafurteile wegen nationalsozialistischer Tötungsverbrechen 1945–1966* (Amsterdam: University Press Amsterdam, 1968–), v. 9, case no. 309.

38 For Kahn's report on Michel and Gerst see Mannheim Gestapo, December 19, 1949, II-419.03, NARA, RG 319, IRR Michel, Franz, D269249.

39 Bischoff, Alois, Reference Card, Agent Report Dated August 4, 1949, and Bischoff, Alois, Reference Card, Agent Report dated December 19, 1949, in NARA, RG 319, IRR Bischoff Alois, D 269231.

40 Bischoff, Alois, Re: Mannheim (L50/M50) Gestapo Activities, April 19, 1950, NARA, RG 319, IRR Bischoff, Alois, D 269231.

41 Ian Sayer and Douglas Botting, *America's Secret Army: The Untold Story of the Counter Intelligence Corps* (London: Grafton, 1989), p. 331.

42 NARA, RG 319, IRR Fischer, Eugen, XE196865.

43 See Mahler's own Fragebogen in NARA, RG 319, IRR Mahler, Anton, XE 050898.

44 Yitzhak Arad, et. al., eds. *The Einsatzgruppen Reports: Selections from the Dispatches of the Nazi Death Squads' Campaign against the Jews in the Occupied Territories of the Soviet Union, July 1941–January 1943* (New York: Holocaust Library, 1989), p. 235.

45 Yitzhak Arad, *The Holocaust in the Soviet Union* (Lincoln; University of Nebraska Press, 2009), p. 55.

46 Mahler, Anton, Case No. 4-2037, NARA, RG 319, IRR Mahler, Anton, D 050898. Memorandum by Lt. Richard Lehr, CIC Screening Staff, undated, NARA, RG 319, IRR Fischer, Eugen, D 112374.

47 L. M. de Riemer (970th CIC Detachment) to Operations Branch, August 26, 1947, NARA, RG 319, IRR Fischer, Eugen, D 112374.

48 Col. David G. Erskine, 66th Counterintelligence Corps (CIC) Detachment to Director, Intelligence Division, HQ, EUCOM, October 12, 1950. See also the request by Maj. Frederick W. Hess of September 9, 1947, and the reply by J. L. McCraw of September 15, 1947; Capt. A. F. Hennings memorandum of September 2, 1947, NARA, RG 319, IRR Fischer, Eugen, D 112374.

49 CIC Region XII November 23, 1949, KPD Activities against Anti-Communist Gestapo Specialists, NARA, RG 319, IRR Fischer, Eugen, D 112374.

50 Special Agent John J. John to HQ, 7970th CIC Group, October 17, 1949, NARA, RG 319, IRR Fischer, Eugen, D 112374.

51 Maj. Henry W. Ida, CIC Region XII to Major George Riggin, HQ 7970 Detachment CIC, October 17, 1949, NARA, RG 319, IRR Fischer, Eugen, D 112374.

52 Mahler, Lebenslauf, May 24, 1949, NARA, RG 319, IRR Mahler, Anton, XE 050898.

53 Bericht Nr. 525, November 12, 1948, NARA, RG 319, IRR Mahler, Anton, XE 050898.

54 CIC Region XII November 23, 1949, KPD Activities against Anti-Communist Gestapo Specialists, NARA, RG 319, IRR Fischer, Eugen, D 112374.

55 Mahler, Lebenslauf, May 24, 1949, NARA, RG 319, IRR Mahler, Anton, XE 050898

56 On his work for Fischer see Col. David G. Erskine, 66th CIC Detachment to Director, Intelligence Division, HQ, EUCOM, October 12, 1950, NARA, RG 319, IRR Fischer, Eugen, D 112374. On his meetings with Berchtold and payments see the payment sheets in NARA, RG 319, IRR Mahler, Anton, XE 050898.

57 CIC Region XII November 23, 1949, KPD Activities against Anti-Communist Gestapo Specialists, NARA, RG 319, IRR Fischer, Eugen, D 112374.

58 Col. David G. Erskine, 66th CIC Detachment to Director, Intelligence Division, HQ, EUCOM, October 12, 1950, NARA, RG 319, IRR Fischer, Eugen, D 112374.

59 Special Agent Siegfried Clemens, Notes on Eugen Fischer-Anton Mahler Trial, undated, p. 17, NARA, RG 319, IRR Fischer, Eugen, D 112374.

60 The judgment dated and signed March 14, 1950, is Aktz. 1 KLa 87–88/49 (III 14/49), in NARA, RG 319, IRR Fischer, Eugen, D112374.

61 Special Agent Siegfried Clemens, Notes on Eugen Fischer-Anton Mahler Trial, undated, p. 28, NARA, RG 319, IRR Fischer, Eugen, D 112374.

62 Maj. George Riggin to Region IV, February 1, 1950, NARA, RG 319, IRR Fischer, Eugen, D 112374.

63 R. F. Cunningham, Chief Operations Division (Frankfurt) to Director of Intelligence, EUCOM, September 14, 1950, NARA, RG 319, IRR Fischer, Eugen, D 112374.

64 Col. David C. Erskine to Director, Intelligence Division, EUCOM, October 12, 1950, NARA, RG 319, IRR Fischer, Eugen, D 112374.

65 Search for the Former Gestapo Officials Eugen Fischer and Anton Mahler, May 29, 1950, NARA, RG 319, IRR Mahler, Anton, XE 050898.

66 Mahler's pay sheet for January 1950 and the Kolb note are in NARA, RG 319, IRR Mahler, Anton, XE 050898.

67 Mahler to Lappler, December 31, 1951 (provided by Lappler to CIC), NARA, RG 319, IRR, Mahler, Anton, XE 050898.

68 Maj. Harold Bush, CIC Region XII, to HQ, 66th CIC Detachment, January 22, 1952, NARA, RG 319, IRR Mahler, Anton, XE050898.

CHAPTER FOUR

▄▄▄▄▄▄▄▄▄▄▄▄▄▄▄

The CIC and Right-Wing Shadow Politics

Allied intelligence organizations monitored communist parties in postwar Germany and Austria, but they also worried about Nazi resurgence. Many former Wehrmacht and SS officers were involved in political intrigue after the war.[1] Scholarly accounts of such movements exist, but the new CIC records have hundreds of files on such groups. What follows are two examples—the *Bruderschaft* (Brotherhood), a shadow organization in West Germany, and the *Spinne* (Spider) a shadow organization in Austria.

The Bruderschaft

The Bruderschaft (Brotherhood) was a semi-secret postwar organization of perhaps 2,500 right-wing German nationalists. The outlines of the organization are known. It was formed in 1949 in the British occupation zone amongst staff officers from the army's elite Grossdeutschland Division, former SS officers, and senior Nazi party members who had been held in England after the war. It worked behind the scenes of West German politics. It maintained ties with right-wing parties and groups in West Germany and with neo-Fascists and ex-Nazis abroad, advocating a Europe independent of either the United States or the USSR, and disintegrated owing to internal fights in 1951. Its significance lay within the rearmament debate in West Germany in 1950 and 1951.

The Bruderschaft's effect was marginal, but the threat it represented for Atlantic security earned it close surveillance by the U.S. Army Counterintelligence Corps (CIC), which discovered the organization after its first meeting in Hamburg in July 1949. The CIC quickly developed sources within the organization. Some 1,500 to 2,000 new pages on the Bruderschaft have now been released. CIC surveillance revealed how badly compromised some of its leaders were, while revealing a fuller picture of the organization's overall strategy and personality feuds.

The Bruderschaft had two leaders. One was SS Col. Alfred Franke-Gricksch. He joined the Nazi Party in 1926 and the SS in 1935. He served as an intelligence officer in the SS Death's Head Division in 1939 and in 1943 moved to the Reich Security Main Office (RSHA) Personnel Office (Amt I) first as Personal Adjutant to Maximilian von Herff and then as the head of the office. In 1943 Franke-Gricksch traveled through occupied Poland, visiting the camps of Auschwitz and Maidanek and witnessing the suppression of the Warsaw Ghetto uprising. He marveled at the wealth collected from Jewish ghettos as well as Auschwitz's efficiency in disposing of Jews.[2] Even in April 1945 he remained a true believer calling for a renewal of Nazi concepts, this time by a group of elite leaders rather than a single man.[3] He was in British captivity from 1945 to 1948, during which time he provided information for MI6.[4] He then returned to his castle near Bielefeld and worked to implement his vision through the political system.

The other leader was Maj. Helmut Beck-Broichsitter, an ex-staff officer from the Grossdeutschland division, who had a reputation as "one of the best qualified young General Staff [sic] Officers in the German Army."[5] Beck-Broichsitter joined the Army in August 1939, serving in Poland, France, Greece, and the USSR. But he joined the Nazi Party in 1931, was a member of the SA in 1932, and a member of the police until 1939. As an Army officer from 1939 to 1944, he served in a variety of field gendarme units, which helped to combat partisans behind German lines. This placed him in the category of automatic arrest.[6]

Other leaders in the Bruderschaft were more notorious. Karl Kaufmann was one of the Nazi Party's earliest members (1922). He was the party Gauleiter in Hamburg from 1929 to 1945 and Hamburg's governor (Reichsstatthalter) from 1933 to 1945. From a stolen Jewish villa, he ran one of Germany's most corrupt administrations, wherein Jewish property and capital rewarded supporters. In

September 1941 Kaufmann became the first city official to deport Jews to occupied Poland. He protected himself after the war with the myth that he opposed the Gestapo, that he lived a modest life on a modest salary, and that he tried to minimize anti-Jewish measures in Hamburg. The British arrested him in May 1945, but Kaufmann was released for health reasons in October 1948. By 1950 CIC knew him as a "bad type" who "controls a group of former NSDAP members."[7]

A January 1950 story in the *New York Herald Tribune* alerted the public to the Bruderschaft. It painted the Bruderschaft as a shadow general staff that provided advice to West German Chancellor Konrad Adenauer through Gen. Hasso von Manteuffel, the Grossdeutschland Division's commander for much of 1944 and one of Adenauer's informal advisers on rearmament. Could the Bruderschaft have signaled that a reconstituted Wehrmacht might overturn the new German democracy?[8] Though Manteuffel publicly denied Bruderschaft membership (many sources said he was a member), the press in both Germanys registered concerns. U.S. High Commissioner John McCloy responded that Allied agents were studying the group.[9]

The CIC began investigating the Bruderschaft in July 1949 with mail intercepts after learning of a secret meeting in Hamburg. The British shared intelligence from their zone. They cryptically revealed that Franke-Gricksch was a "high-category Nazi who was released under certain restrictions" but "failed to live up to the conditions of his release."[10] The CIC recruited its own more moderate sources from within the Bruderschaft. These included Col. Eberhard Graf von Nostitz, a former staff officer from the 2nd Panzer Army and close friend of Manteuffel. He worked for British intelligence, with a net that included former Foreign Office and Gestapo personnel, and also worked for the Gehlen Organization. Though he, like Manteuffel, denied membership in the Bruderschaft, he maintained frequent contact with its members and attended its meetings.[11]

Centered in Hamburg, the Bruderschaft was strongest in the British zone, but it also had members in the French, U.S., and Soviet zones. Its overt aims were easy to learn, since Beck-Broichsitter spoke with Allied authorities and the press. These aims reflected well-worn army officers' thinking: anti-Soviet and pro-Western policies that also called for the rehabilitation of German soldiers through restored state pensions and the release of officers from war crimes enclosures. Beck-Broichsitter told U.S. High Commission members that the

Soviets aimed at "the Bolshevization of Western Germany and Western Europe through phony peace initiatives and the offer of German unity." The United States, he said, should counter Soviet efforts. "It had been Germany's historic mission during the past 1,000 years," he said "to defend the Occident against Russian onslaughts."[12] Beck-Broichsitter further noted that the officer class "feel that their honor has been insulted by the mass arrests and other indignities they have endured as an aftermath of World War II."[13]

The Bruderschaft's covert aims were more dangerous. A CIA assessment of August 1950 noted "the implications of the covert program, together with the political backgrounds of the leaders and most of the members, leave little doubt that the organization espouses neo-Nazism, with changes from the Nazi program dictated by an opportunistic appraisal of the present international situation."[14] The Bruderschaft insisted that the Federal Republic and its constitution were illegitimate Allied-imposed structures. Karl Dönitz, Hitler's successor who surrendered militarily to the Allies in May 1945 and was now serving a prison sentence, never surrendered state power. "Under these circumstances," read a secret Bruderschaft statement of February 1950, "the [former] German state must be considered as still in existence." The Bruderschaft favored dictatorship by elite officers: "We hope," said the statement, "that the era of the masses has passed, and that the moment for the development of the elite has come."[15]

The Bruderschaft aimed to create such a condition by forging right-wing party coalitions, placing its members in key government positions, and exercising influence behind the scenes. Intercepted correspondence from 1949 revealed that Beck-Broichsitter tried to forge a CDU-Deutsche Partei coalition in Schleswig-Holstein to maximize the right-wing vote there.[16] In November 1950 Beck-Broichsitter talked of a "National Representation" of right-wing parties, including the neo-Nazi Socialist Reich Party (SRP) which "would form a state within a state and would be independent of both the Bonn Government and the Government of East Germany." British sources said that former Gen. Heinz Guderian, the famous tank commander who served as Hitler's loyal army chief-of-staff in 1944 and 1945, agreed to lead the National Representation.[17] Franke-Gricksch said privately that parliamentary government in West Germany would collapse by 1953 and that there were "sufficient qualified men within the Bruderschaft's ranks to take over the entire administration of Germany."[18] The CIA noted "several instances of lower-level relationships between the Bruderschaft and regional officials of the federal coalition parties...."[19] There was no evidence that the Bruderschaft influenced government policy but some members, including Manteuffel, had access to senior figures.[20]

The Bruderschaft's covert foreign aims included an armed independent European force under German leadership, as anti-American as it was anti-Soviet. It thus rejected German membership in NATO. As special agent Edward Hoffer noted, the Bruderschaft was "not pro-Allied. They are simply pro-Deutsch, and against any form of east or west occupation or protection." They even rejected the Gehlen Organization's work under ostensible U.S. supervision.[21] Guderian said in August 1950 that he would "rather raise the pistol to both the Americans and the Russians at the same time," but for the impracticality of such a step.[22] "The covert program," according to the CIA,

> projects a united Europe in which Germany would presumably play the leading role by virtue of its size, power, and position. This Europe would withdraw from close political and military cooperation with the US and, although opposing international Bolshevism and Soviet interference in European affairs, could take a neutral position between the US and USSR or even enter as an equal partner into alliance with the USSR. The authoritarian government envisioned for Germany, despite Bruderschaft claims that it is against Fascism and dictatorship, would presumably be extended to the other European countries through the foreign neo-fascists with whom the Bruderschaft maintains contact.[23]

Finally, the Bruderschaft insisted on restoration of Germany's 1937 boundaries, which its members believed could be attained with timely lies to the Soviets and Americans alike. The Poles, who had benefited most from border readjustments in 1945, would not be consulted.[24]

How were the covert aims to be brought about? The Bruderschaft maintained close ties with like-minded Germans from former Nazis to Ruhr industrialists as well as right-wing groups throughout Western Europe. Franke-Gricksch was in frequent touch with British Fascist Oswald Mosley, and Beck-Broichsitter claimed to have met Pope Pius XII. "The Catholic Church is very interested in our movement," Beck-Broichsitter said, "because we represent the first line of defense against Bolshevism."[25] Franke-Gricksch also cultivated contacts in the East Germany. These included secret Bruderschaft members with whom Franke-Gricksch maintained courier nets. They also included members of the Socialist Unity Party and the Soviet Military Administration. Franke-Gricksch hoped that Moscow's various statements on German unity in return for "peace"—whatever this might mean to the Soviets—might be used to good effect.[26]

In August 1950 Karl Kaufmann talked of "primarily siding with the Russians, and later turning against them in order to reestablish the old Germany."[27] In March 1951, Franke-Gricksch argued that "Germany should pretend to collaborate with the East until certain concessions are granted by the West, then shift toward the West to gain concessions from the East."[28] In November 1950, he told the Americans through Günther d'Alquen (the former editor of the SS magazine *Das Schwarze Korps*) that "the Americans sooner or later will be compelled to turn to the Bruderschaft for assistance...."[29] In fact, Franke-Gricksch's relationships in East Germany opened the Bruderschaft up to penetration by communist agents.[30]

What could be done about the Bruderschaft? Adenauer's top military advisers, Gen. Adolf Heusinger and Gen. Hans Speidel, viewed the Bruderschaft as "young, overambitious, ex-officers" who comprised a "radical right wing group" with a "liberal sprinkling of SS elements" who "became bitter over their fate after the war and decided that their life under Hitler wasn't so bad after all." According to the British, Manteuffel and other senior army officers in the Bruderschaft were mostly interested in restoring the Wehrmacht's good name and were "horrified by the public exposure of their names as leaders of an underground movement in association with those of ex-Gauleiters and SS leaders." Equally uncomfortable with Franke-Gricksch's Communist ties, they hoped to reorganize the Bruderschaft along more conservative lines in 1950. Heusinger and Speidel argued that state pensions for officers and the release of Army personnel from war crimes enclosures would satisfy ex-officers and help the Bruderschaft to "die a natural death."[31]

In fact, the Bruderschaft died even before such developments owing to splits between Franke-Gricksch and Beck-Broichsitter. Disagreements over strategy were decisive. By 1951 Beck-Broichsitter and the military clique, though still hoping for military independence, advocated cooperation with the United States and rejected connections with the USSR. Franke-Griksch's backers believed a pro-Soviet policy offered the best chance for German unity and that "One cannot trust the words of [NATO Commander] Eisenhower since he remains what he has always been, namely a German hater."[32] In a bitter meeting of February 1951 Franke-Gricksch accused Beck-Broichsitter of spying on the Bruderschaft for the Bundesamt für Verfassungsschutz (BfV), West Germany's domestic intelligence agency. Beck-Broichsitter resigned from his leadership post rather than undergo a trial by the Bruderschaft's honor court. The CIC later established that he had a relationship with the BfV, which was surely interested in Franke-Gricksch's connections with East Germany and the Soviets.[33]

After his ouster in February 1951, Beck-Broichsitter took the Bruderschaft factions from the French occupation zone and from Baden-Württemberg in the U.S. zone, and renamed his group the Bruderschaft Deutschland. Ostensibly he rejected cooperation with former Nazi figures, but in July 1951 he appointed Erich Bujalla, a former Gestapo officer from Bremen, as his local designate in Frankfurt. Bujalla pledged to "use a definite National Socialist spirit in leading the Frankfurt Bruderschaft." He quickly recruited old Nazi police friends for the Bruderschaft Deutschland.[34] For the rest, Beck-Broichsitter maintained contact with Hans Speidel during the rearmament debates, advocating a paramilitary program for German boys under the Bruderschaft Deutschland that included marching, reconnaissance, and the like. He increasingly became a non-factor as West Germany remilitarized, joined NATO, and saw its ex-Wehrmacht officers released from Allied prisons.[35] Franke-Gricksch continued to build the Bruderschaft. But in October 1951, during a trip to East Germany, he was arrested and tried for war crimes in the USSR. He reportedly died in a Soviet prison camp in 1953.[36]

The Spider

Previously released CIC materials contained spotty information on Austria thanks partly to the scattered and fragmentary nature of the operational records of the 430th CIC Detachment, which monitored the U.S. occupation zone there.[37] The most interesting material thus far has been the lengthy personal file of Wilhelm Höttl, a SD officer who served in Hungary in 1944 and who created two intelligence nets for the CIC in 1948.[38] The new records contain more information on such activity. The tale of an organization called the Spinne (Spider) serves as an example.

The Spinne is the stuff of legend. It was "uncovered" in 1949 by the American journalist Curt Reiss who wrote that Goebbels's subordinate Dr. Johannes Leers stood at its head. In the 1960s it was said to be a secret organization of former Nazis with high contacts in West Germany that helped war criminals escape to the Middle East, South Africa, and elsewhere.[39] The true Spinne was actually a secret association of Austrian Nazis who in 1949 pressed for the rehabilitation of Austrian Nazis and for a pan-German agenda that included a second Anschluss with a reunited Germany. Its significance lies in the Austrian national election of October 1949.

Austria had roughly 700,000 Nazis when the war ended. In May 1945 Austria's new government legally banned the Nazi organizations, prohibited former Nazis from voting and state employment, and required all Nazis to register (about 524,000 did so). A War Criminals Law of June 1945 established People's Courts throughout Austria that heard some 136,000 cases and pronounced 13,607 guilty verdicts over the next decade.[40] The National Socialist Law of February 1947 established categories of Nazis including war criminals (including illegal Nazis from the 1933 to 1938 period); "incriminated" Nazis (SS and Gestapo members for instance); and "less-incriminated" Nazis. A law of April 1948 amnestied "less-incriminated" Nazis (about 550,000 persons), allowing them to vote. With only 2.5 million voters in Austria, this group and their families were an important voting bloc.[41]

The four occupying powers initially licensed three political parties in Austria. The Austrian People's Party (Österreichische Volkspartei—ÖVP) represented Catholic conservatives. The Social Democratic Party of Austria (Sozialdemokratische Partei Österreichs—SPÖ) and the Communist Party of Austria (Kommunistische Partei Österreichs—KPÖ) represented the moderate and extreme left. The ÖVP and SPÖ formed an anti-Communist coalition government in 1945. But was a coalition between conservatives and social democrats the only anti-Communist alternative? Might a more rightist alternative be attractive to former Nazis in 1949?

Herbert Kraus was the main figure vying for the votes of former Nazis. Born in Zagreb in 1911, Kraus was a German economic official in the Ukraine from 1941 to 1943 who was removed for speaking against German policies. He then served in a combat intelligence unit. He emerged after the war in Salzburg where he lived in the renovated Schloss Frohnberg (later made famous in *The Sound of Music*).

Kraus formed a private think tank in Salzburg called the Österreichische Forschungsinstitut für Wirtschaft und Politik, which conducted public opinion polls and reported news and opinion in a weekly called *Berichte und Informationen*. He also had a relationship with CIC, having turned over various SS personalities to U.S. authorities after the war and having helped create four intelligence operations including Project Jackpot, aimed at the KPÖ. *Berichte and Informationen* was highly critical of the Soviets but also complained about the "punitive" nature of denazification in Austria, which prevented a more "spiritual denazification" and the joining of Austria with the western bloc of nations. The CIC viewed Kraus as reliable and pro-American, with "mild rightist tendencies."[42] The CIC's operations chief in Salzburg, Maj. James V. Milano, noted in 1948 that up to one-third of the Army's intelligence efforts in Austria depended on Krause.[43] In fact, his research institute might have had an intelligence-gathering function.[44]

In February 1949 Kraus formed a fourth political party called the League of Independents (Verband der Unabhänginge—VdU). It was a non-religious party committed to free markets that aimed to attract the uncommitted 30 percent of the Austrian electorate, including "intellectual Nazis," right-wing Socialists, and conservative independents, all of which, he felt, could produce 1.5 million votes.[45] Kraus hoped he could form a right-wing coalition with the ÖVP. The Spinne was an organization of former war criminals and other "implicated" Nazis. They could neither vote nor serve in state office, and they faced possible criminal charges. They aimed to take over the VdU from within and govern from behind the scenes afterwards. Austrian historian Lothar Höbelt dismisses the Spinne entirely in his apologetic history of the VdU.[46]

The CIC first learned of the Spinne in September 1949 after the ÖVP began an anti-VdU press campaign aimed at maintaining ÖVP vote totals.[47] In an extensive investigation CIC special agents interviewed VdU functionaries who had resigned from the party, intercepted and transcribed telephone calls to and from VdU leaders, and studied key VdU documents. One of the informants was Karl von Winkler, a former Abwehr major who had worked against the Nazis in Austria and who was a founding member of the VdU, hoping that it might become a legitimate nationalist party.[48] Another was Hans Georg von Schwarzkopf, Kraus's private secretary, who was a reliable U.S. informant, providing extensive information on Kraus, the VdU, and its Nazi supporters.[49]

The Spinne initially formed in U.S. Detention Camp Marcus W. Orr in Glanzenbach near Salzburg. This camp held more Nazi officials than any other enclosure in Austria, some 12,000 in all.[50] It was a hothouse of unreconstructed Nazism and political intrigue. The CIC had an agent within the camp and a number of informants including von Schwarzkopf. "The inmates of Camp Orr," reported CIC Special Agent F. K. Richter, "regarded themselves as the elite of Austria, and they were firmly convinced that Austrian recovery depended entirely upon their release…. They felt absolutely certain that they would regain their power, staff the government with experts rather than 'politicians,' and establish a new and better National Socialist regime [,] naturally avoiding the errors made by Hitler and his 'false advisors.'"[51] Members of the Spinne organization, according to various informants, swore "an oath of loyalty and solidarity" and were "devoted to the re-establishment of their personal power." The name Spinne referred to "a centrally located body… and a web, reaching to all National Socialists and into all Allied Intelligence Services."[52] Camp Orr officially closed in August 1948.

The leaders of the Spinne were Erich Kernmayer and Karl Kowarik, both implicated Austrian Nazis. Kernmayer joined the Nazi Party and the SA in 1934, when both were illegal in Austria. After the Anschluss in 1938 he became the editor of the formerly anti-Nazi periodical *Deutsche Telegraf*. From 1939 to 1940 he was the press chief for Gauleiter Joseph Bürckel of Vienna, during a period of intense anti-Jewish violence, expropriation, and expulsion there. When Bürckel became Gauleiter in the Westmark (the Saar, Bavarian Palatinate, and Lorraine), Kernmayer again became his press chief. In 1941 during Germany's invasion of Greece, Kernmayer was assigned to the Leibstandarte Adolf Hitler as a war propagandist. Later service took him to the USSR, to Hungary, and ultimately in 1945, to American captivity.[53] In Camp Orr, Kernmayer broadcast news analysis over the public address system. His anti-Soviet comments predicted imminent war between the United States and the USSR. A CIC agent in the camp, Special Agent F. K. Richter, suspected that Kernmayer was behind the murder of Professor Alois Koch in March 1947 for Koch's collaboration with the Americans.[54]

Karl Kowarik was another Vienna Nazi who joined the Party in 1930. He became the Hitler Youth leader in Vienna in 1934 and eventually all of Austria. Described as "an old National Socialist of outstanding conviction," he became an SS officer in 1939.[55] According to one CIC agent, Kowarik was one of Camp Orr's most violent Nazis, "a man who would have been nothing save for the Nazis, and who could never be expected to give up his National Socialist convictions."[56]

Kernmayer and Kowarik were released from Camp Orr in 1947. They found work as operations chiefs in the CIC intelligence nets created by Wilhelm Höttl in 1948. The CIC dropped both nets in 1949 owing to their unreliability. But Kernmayer continued to find work as a U.S. intelligence source while also writing an anti-Semitic apologia for Nazism published in Switzerland entitled *Die grosse Rausch* (The Great Intoxication, 1948), which sold 12,000 copies in Austria within three months (the Allies later banned sales of the book in Austria).[57] It was the first of a number of books in which Kernmayer glorified the Nazi past. CIC agents in Salzburg protected Kernmayer. In 1948 Austrian authorities arrested him for trial in Linz. CIC officials "advised the Austrian judicial authorities to take no further action in the pending case until further advised by the American authorities," then asked them to halt prosecution altogether. As late as January 1949, Kernmayer was still connected with a CIC network, and as late as 1952, the CIC reported that he was "selling spurious intelligence reports to intelligence agencies in Austria" regarding Soviet activities.[58]

Kernmayer and Kowarik supported themselves through peddling intelligence. But they wanted political power, and Kraus's VdU was the perfect vehicle. Kernmayer might have known Kraus from his time in Camp Orr. His broadcasts were culled from Kraus's *Berichte und Informationen*. In 1948 Kernmayer approached Kraus, introducing him to Camp Orr's leading Nazis who were looking for a "political mouthpiece." According to Kraus's secretary Hans Georg Schwartzkopf, "the Nazis fed Dr. Kraus' ambition and vanity" and the "entire organization of the VdU was submitted to Dr. Kraus by these Nazis."[59] Another source noted that, "from the very beginning [Kernmayer] told Dr. Herbert A. Kraus that he [Kernmayer] was the man who could lead the great mass of the former Nazis into the VdU."[60]

When he announced his plans to form the VdU in February 1949, Kraus, according to CIC sources, stated that he "intended to recruit the million votes now controlled by former Nazis and their families."[61] Such would give him 40 percent of the vote. "The Nazis will not run my Party," Kraus told former German intelligence official Hans Gostentschnigg, "we need them only to increase our votes and our membership."[62] "He stated to me," said Hans Georg Schwarzkopf, "that the VdU could not exist without the Nazis and that he had to be careful not to let the Nazis deprive him of his own power at some later time."[63]

How did Kraus plan to control the Nazis within his party? The CIC learned that Kraus "proposed to use alleged non-implicated Nazis who enjoy the fullest confidence of the former National Socialists to secure this voting block [sic]."[64] But the implicated Nazis had different plans. The initial general meeting of the VdU on March 26, 1949, included implicated Nazis, and according to Schwarzkopf, it took place in an atmosphere reminiscent of "old-time Nazi gatherings. The old National Socialists present were determined to gain the upper hand." A few non-Nazis, such as Kraus himself, occupied senior positions, but it was "only the agreement of the Nazis which [allowed Kraus] to maintain his position as chairman of the VdU." U.S. authorities reported that "While the VdU is ostensibly a democratic and non-Nazi party operating under the slogan of 'decency' (Anstaendigkeit), and was probably originally intended as such by its founder, Dr. Kraus, it could not maintain such a direction for very long, because of the National Socialist advisors with whom Dr. Kraus surrounded himself. Dr. Kraus is considered to be a very pliable man…."[65]

Kernmayer placed Spinne members in the VdU's national administration and, according to the Austrian authorities, they constantly reported back to him.[66] His network included Franz Pesendorfer who belonged to the SS Standarte 89 in Vienna, responsible for the 1934 murder of Chancellor Engelbert Dolfuss. Pesendorfer led the VdU's press office.[67] Felix Rinner, another former member of SS Standarte 89, told a CIC informant in 1949 that "I work for the VdU in Vienna because it is 'our' party… I am not a member of the VdU but I devote all of my time to informing our people that they must vote only for the VdU. We are a completely right-wing party and we hope to constitute a two-third majority in Austria, together with the ÖVP."[68] Numerous sources placed Höttl within the Spinne as the VdU's intelligence chief. As Austrian police authorities told the Americans, "Kernmayer and Kowarik hope that they can get rid of Dr. Kraus without any difficulties; they are waiting only for the moment in which the Nazis, through the VdU, will get … a voice in parliament, in order to show their demands and carry them out."[69] Already on September 20, telephone intercepts revealed calls to Kraus with warnings such as "we do not agree with your program, change it." Special Agent Roger E. Lankford concluded that, "the 'Spider Group' is a group of ex-high Nazis who are hopeful of regaining political power in the future; that they are actually the 'power behind the thrown [sic]' as far as the VdU is concerned; that they are actually giving Kraus … all orders."[70]

What was the VdU agenda? According to Schwarzkopf, "Dr. Kraus and his VdU are completely pan-German in their orientation." They favored a united Germany joined with Austria. Kraus had frequent meetings with members of the Deutsche Union in Germany, particularly former Wehrmacht officers, who, according to Schwarzkopf, "look upon the founding of the VdU as a trial run for a similar movement in Germany." Kraus, meanwhile, was sure that the VdU would gain at least 30 percent of the vote and that even ÖVP and SPÖ functionaries would defect to the VdU shortly before the election. The victory, he said, would be "of landslide proportions." VdU intelligence officers including Höttl were "almost exclusively Nazis," who followed the tactics to undermine the Austrian government that had proven successful in 1938.[71] Karl von Winkler told CIC investigators that "…the VdU, as it stands today and has always stood, is pan-German and antisemitic in intent … Dr. Kraus is completely swayed by his Nazi advisors."[72]

As the October 1949 elections drew closer, others showed increased concern. Andreas Rohrbacher, the Archbishop of Salzburg, with whom Kraus had been friendly, now admonished Kraus. "Your party," said the Archbishop, "will materially weaken the conservative front and thus increase the power of the leftist parties.… I have misgivings about some points of your program, which sound rather radical, and then also because of the incorrigible Nazis … you are providing cover for a group of people now who, sooner or later, will show their real face…."[73]

The ÖVP launched a press campaign against the VdU hinting that Kraus was a CIC agent and that his party was a front for a Nazi resurgence. The CIC worried that Kraus and other intelligence contacts would be compromised. "Such a campaign," wrote Major Milano, "can be a serious blow to US intelligence as well as result in the loss of a large financial investment. Dr. Krause [sic] is definitely a long-range proposition." Milano also worried that Krause could retaliate against the ÖVP's own intelligence connections that had a Nazi taint. The entire feud could have major repercussions, which, according to Maj. J. V. Milano, could "kill one third of the USFA [what is this organization?] intelligence effort…."[74]

Instead, the CIC managed its own campaign. Dr. Gustav Canaval was the conservative editor of the *Salzburger Nachrichten*, the first licensed newspaper in the U.S. zone of Austria. He had been a friend of Kurt von Schusschnigg, the Austrian Chancellor ousted by Hitler, and he was the editor of the *Deutsche Telegraf* in 1938 when Kernmayer took it over. He thus had a score to settle.[75] Canaval launched an anti-VdU press campaign, partially funded by the Austrian government. Canaval even coordinated with the World Jewish Congress (WJC), and, with the help of U.S. contacts, he published translated versions of WJC articles sent to French, Swiss, and U.S. news agencies about the VdU. The CIC kept its role invisible to avoid compromising its relationship with anyone who might be "possible future sources of information."[76]

In the October 1949 national election, the VdU gained only 11.7 percent of the national vote and 16 parliamentary seats out of 165. The SPÖ remained the ÖVP's coalition partners. The VdU's share of the vote was the strongest showing by an alternative right-wing party until Jörg Haider's victory of 1990, but the party fell into dissension in 1952. It disintegrated by 1955. Kernmayer continued his dubious writing career under the pseudonym Erich Kern, maintained contacts with old SS colleagues, and continued to sell "spurious intelligence reports" on the Soviets to various agencies in Austria.[77] Kraus resigned as VdU chairman in 1952. In the meantime he continued to work as an anti-Communist agitator and established liaisons with French and German right-wing groups interested in European unity. Included among his contacts in 1950 were leading members of the Bruderschaft in Germany.[78]

NOTES

1 The best summary in English is Martin A. Lee, *The Beast Reawakens* (Boston: Little Brown, 1997).

2 His report is excerpted in Gerald Fleming, *Hitler and the Final Solution* (Berkeley, CA: University of California Press, 1984), pp. 142–43.

3 Gerhard Förster, Richard Lakowski: *1945: Das Jahr der endgültigen Niederlage der faschistischen Wehrmacht. Dokumente.* 2nd ed. (Berlin: Militärverlag, 1985), p. 239.

4 Stephen Dorrill, *MI6: Inside the Covert World of Her Majesty's Secret Service* (New York: Free Press, 2002), p. 103.

5 Special Agent Ibo Hecht, Region XII, 66th CIC Detachment, Die Bruderschaft, September 29, 1950, NARA, RG 319, IRR Die Bruderschaft v. 1, D 267740.

6 For Beck-Broichsitter's CIC file see NARA, RG 319, IRR, Beck-Brochsitter, Helmut, D 119321.

7 On Hamburg see Frank Bajohr, "Gauleiter in Hamburg: Zur Person und Tätigkeit Karl Kaufmanns, *Vierteljahrshefte für Zeitgeschichte*, v. 43, n. 2 (April 1995), p. 272. On his postwar apologetics and CIC comments see NARA, RG 319, IRR, Kaufmann, Karl, D 002645.

8   "Ex-General Advises Adenauer to Get Infantry, Panzer Units," *New York Herald Tribune*, January 4, 1950. Clipping in NARA, RG 319, IRR Die Bruderschaft, D 267241.

9   On Manteuffel's membership, see "Bruderschaft," *Der Spiegel*, March 2, 1950; Special Agent Fritz Weinschens, report of March 17, 1950, NARA, RG 319, IRR Die Bruderschaft Factions, D 267240. For press, see "West German Military Group Being Studied," *New York Herald Tribune*, February 2, 1950. Clipping in NARA, RG 319, IRR, Die Bruderschaft, D 267241. The Soviet press organ *Tägliche Rundschau*, reported that U.S. intelligence "actively encouraged" the *Bruderschaft*. "Hitler-Generale: Ein Glied der USA-Armee, *Tägliche Rundschau*, February 23, 1950, NARA, RG 319, IRR, Die Bruderschaft, D 267241. On Manteuffel's relationship with Adenauer, see David Clay Large, *Germans to the Front: West German Rearmament in the Adenauer Era* (Chapel Hill, NC, University of North Carolina Press, 1993), pp. 50, 138, 243.

10 Allen J. Hoden, Memorandum of February 13, 1950, NARA, RG 319, IRR Die Bruderschaft, D 267241.

11 Col. David Erskine (HQ, CIC 66th Detachment) to Commanding Officer, Region X, MSG No. 10, February 20, 1950, NARA, RG 319, IRR Die Bruderschaft, D 267241; CIC Region II to HH, 66th CIC Detachment, December 7, 1950, NARA, RG 319, IRR, D 267240. Also cards of November 10, 1950, November 15, 1950, and December 20, 1950, NARA, RG 319, IRR, Nostitz, Eberhard Graf von XE 020327 and D 020327.

12 Report by Kenneth Dayton, Chief, Internal Political and Government Affairs Division, HICOG-Frankfurt, No. 1188, Date Illegible, NARA, RG 319, IRR Die Bruderschaft v. 1, D 267740.

13 Headquarters Region V, 66th CIC Detachment, Organizational Summary Report [on the Bruderschaft in Regensburg], September 14, 1950, NARA, RG 319, IRR Die Bruderschaft, v. 1, D 267740.

14 Central Intelligence Agency, Intelligence Memorandum No. 281, August 15, 1950, NARA, RG 319, IRR Die Bruderschaft, D 267740.

15 Quoted in Secret Report on the *Bruderschaft*, Enclosure to HICOG Frankfurt 969, June 7, 1950, NARA, RG 319, IRR Die Bruderschaft v. 1, D 267740.

16 Extract from SITREP No. 19 for Week Ending 3 November 1949, NARA, RG 319, IRR Die Bruderschaft, D 267241; Col. David Erskine (HQ, CIC 66th Detachment) to CIC Liaison Officer for Analysis Branch, MSG No. 1, February 20, 1950, NARA, RG 319, IRR Die Bruderschaft, D 267241.

17 Directorate of Security Contribution to Intelligence Division Top Secret Summary for November 1950, November 28, 1950, NARA, RG 319, IRR Die Bruderschaft Factions, D 267240. On the relationship with the SRP, see Special Agent Arnold C. Vollem, CIC Region IX, December 21, 1950, NARA, RG 319, IRR Die Bruderschaft Factions, D 267240.

18 Special Agent Bronislaw F. Gmyr, Region I, 66th CIC Detachment, Die Bruderschaft, October 23, 1950, NAA, RG 319 Die Bruderschaft v. 1, IRR, D 267740.

19 Central Intelligence Agency, Intelligence Memorandum No. 281, August 15, 1950, NARA, RG 319, IRR Die Bruderschaft v. 1, D 267740.

20 Special Agent Leo Hecht, Region XII, 66th CIC Detachment, Die Bruderschaft, September 29, 1950, NARA, RG 319, IRR Die Bruderschaft v. 1, D 267740. Contrast with CIC Region II to HQ 66th CIC Detachment, December 7, 1950, NARA, RG 319, IRR Die Bruderschaft v. 1, D 267240.

21 Special Agent Edward W. Hoffer, Special Team Report #33, September 13, 1950, NARA, RG 319, IRR Die Bruderschaft v. 1, D 267740.

22 Headquarters Region V, 66th CIC Detachment, Organizational Summary Report [on the Bruderschaft in Regensburg], September 14, 1950, NARA, RG 319, IRR Die Bruderschaft v. 1, D 267740. This report has Guderian as a member of the *Herrenklub*, a loose organization of high-ranking officers, and as a spokesman for the *Bruderschaft*. Guderian had ties with numerous underground right-wing groups and there are several U.S. Army Counterintelligence files on him that include mail surveillance in the new records. See NARA, RG 319, IRR Guderian, Heinz, XE 010802, vols. 1–5.

23 Central Intelligence Agency, Intelligence Memorandum No. 281, August 15, 1950, NARA, RG 319, IRR Die Bruderschaft v. 1, D 267740.

24 Secret Report on the Bruderschaft, Enclosure to HICOG Frankfurt 969, June 7, 1950, NARA, RG 319, IRR Die Bruderschaft v. 1, D 267740; "Notes on West German Security," July 1950, in Special Agent Eugene Kolb, report Views on Remilitarization, August 1950, NARA, RG 319, IRR Die Bruderschaft v. 1, D 267740.

25 Special Agent Fritz Weinschens, report of March 17, 1950, NARA, RG 319, IRR Die Bruderschaft Factions, D 267240. On Franke-Gricksch's relationship with Mosley, see Graham Macklin, *Very Deeply Dyed in Black: Sir Oswald Mosley and the Resurrection of British Fascism after 1945* (New York: Taurus, 2007), pp. 91–93. Contacts with Countess Lili Hamilton, Bishop Alois Hudal, fighter pilot Hans-Ulrich Rudel, former SS Lt. Col. Otto Skorzeny and others are mentioned throughout the CIC *Bruderschaft* files. CIC information also pointed to continued contact between Franke-Gricksch and "British friends from the Secret Service." See Franke-Gricksch, Alfred, Consolidated Information Collected from CPI Cards as of April 18, 1951, NARA, RG 319, IRR Die Bruderschaft Factions, D 267240.

26 Franke-Gricksch said that there were 600 *Bruderschaft* members in East Germany and that some even occupied important positions in the East German *Volkspolizei*. On the *Bruderschaft*'s relationship with East Germany and the Soviet Military Administration see CO, CIC, Region II to HQ 66th CIC Detachment, December 5, 1950, NARA, RG 319, IRR Die Bruderschaft Factions, D 267240; CIC Region X to HQ, 66th CIC Detachment, December 18, 1950, NARA, RG 319, IRR Die Bruderschaft Factions, D 267240; Special Agent John D. Schlichtman, CIC Region II, January 10, 1951, NARA, RG 319, IRR, D 267240; Special Agent Lloyd R. Mabrey, Region II, 66th CIC Detachment, Bruderschaft Negotiations with the Soviet Military Administration, September 27, 1950, NARA, RG 319, IRR Die Bruderschaft v. 1, D 267740. On Stalin and German unity after 1945, see Gerhard Wettig, *Stalin and the Cold War in Europe: The Emergence and Development of East-West Conflict, 1939–1953* (Lanham, MD: Rowman and Littlefield, 2008), pp. 201–41.

27 Special Agent Bronislaw F. Gmyr, Region I, 66th CIC Detachment, Die Bruderschaft, October 23, 1950, NAA, RG 319, IRR Die Bruderschaft v. 1, D 267740.

28 Special Agents Bronislaw F. Gmyr and August A. Boelter, CIC Region I, March 16, 1951, NARA, RG 319, IRR Die Bruderschaft Factions, D 267240.

29 Lt. Col. C. N. Coleman, HQ, 66th CIC Detachment Region IV, to HQ, 66th CIC Detachment, November 10, 1950, NARA, RG 319, IRR Die Bruderschaft Factions, D 267240.

30 James H. Critchfield, *Partners at the Creation: The Men Behind Postwar Germany's Defense and Intelligence Establishments* (Annapolis, MD: U.S. Naval Institute Press, 2003), p. 121.

31 On Heusinger and Speidel, see Activities of Former German Officer Groups, March 14, 1950, NARA, RG 319, IRR Die Bruderschaft, D 267241. On Manteuffel, British Intelligence Summary #26, April 1950, NARA, RG 319, IRR Die Bruderschaft Factions, D 267240. On other Army officers see Directorate of Security Contribution to Intelligence Division Top Secret Summary for November 1950, November 28, 1950, NARA, RG 319, IRR Die Bruderschaft Factions, D 267240; Information Report, December 6, 1950, NARA, RG 319, IRR Die Bruderschaft Factions, D 267240.

32 Special Agent John D. Schlichtman, March 5, 1951, NARA, RG 319, IRR Die Bruderschaft Factions, D 267240; Information Report, March 2, 1951, NARA, RG 319, IRR Die Bruderschaft Factions, D 267240; Special Agent John D. Schlichtman, CIC Region II, March 6, 1951, NARA, RG 319, IRR Die Bruderschaft Factions, D 267240.

33 Special Agent Bronislaw F. Gmyr, March 9, 1951, NARA, RG 319, IRR Die Bruderschaft Factions, D 267240. On Beck-Broichsitter's relationship with the BfV, see Special Agent John D. Schlichtman, CIC Region II, May 22, 1951, NARA, RG 319, IRR Die Deutsche Bruderschaft v. 1, D 293797.

34 Special Agents Heinz C. Colbert and Joseph P. Coxedge, July 12, 1951, NARA, RG 319, IRR, D 293797; Special Agents Heinz C. Colbert and Joseph P. Coxedge, July 20, 1951, NARA, RG 319, IRR Die Deutsche Bruderschaft v. 1, D 293797.

35 Extract, April 12, 1951, NARA, RG 319, IRR Die Deutsche Bruderschaft v. 1, D293797; Special Agent John D. Schlichtman, CIC Region II, May 22, 1951, NARA, RG 319, IRR Die Bruderschaft Factions, D267240; Special Agent John D. Schlichtman, CIC Region II, June 1, 1951, NARA, RG 319, IRR Die Bruderschaft Factions, D 267240.

36 Fleming, *Hitler and the Final Solution*, p. 141.

37 Scattered reports for 430th CIC exist but very little of its operational files. [See RGs 165, 260, 319, 332, 338, and 498.]

38 Höttl's CIA Name File has a great deal of CIC material. See Norman J.W. Goda, "The Nazi Peddler: Wilhelm Höttl and Allied Intelligence," in Breitman, et. al., *U.S. Intelligence and the Nazis*, pp. 265–78.

39 "Half Die 'Spinne' bei der Flucht?" *Der Spiegel*, No. 47/1966, p. 87.

40 Figures in Hellmut Butterweck, *Verurteilt und Begnadigt: Österreich und seine NS-Straftäter* (Vienna: Czernin, 2003), p. 13.

41 Heidemarie Uhl, "From Victim Myth to Co-Responsibility Thesis: Nazi Rule, World War II, and the Holocaust in Austrian Memory," in *The Politics of Memory in Postwar Europe*, ed. Richard Ned Lebow, Wulf Kansteiner, and Claudio Fugo (Durham, NC: Duke University Press, 2006), p. 44.

42 Maj. J. V. Milano, to Lieutenant Colonel Carey, Memorandum for the Record, August 9, 1949; Jack E. Heibler, Assistant Chief of Operations, Land Salzburg Sub-Detachment to Chief, CIC, Land Salzburg Detachment, September 10, 1949, NARA, RG 319, IRR Spider, XA 000902. Also Special Agent Harris C. Greene, Memorandum for the Officer in Charge, November 10, 1947, NARA, RG 319, IRR Spider, XA 000902; On *Berichte und Informationen* see the reports in NARA, RG 319, IRR Kraus, Herbert, XA 010790.

43 Maj. J. V. Milano, Memo for the Record, August 10, 1949, NARA, RG 319, IRR Spider, XA 000902.

44 The Austrian Research Institute also had branch offices in Klagenfurt, Graz, Vienna, Innsbruck, Bregenz and Linz. The British authorities in Carinthia thought that the organization had a covert intelligence function, and from the start Kraus created it to be better informed than the Austrian government itself. See Intelligence Organization, Allied Commission for Austria, Ib/I/SF/1400/E, June 5, 1946, NARA, RG 319, IRR Kraus, Herbert, HE 079877; Civil Censorship Group Austria, Salzburg Station, S/T/1008, November 20, 1945, NARA, RG 319, IRR Kraus, Herbert, HE 079877.

45 See the partial report by Special Agent Harris C. Greene, NARA, RG 319, IRR Kraus, Herbert, XA 010790. See also Max Riedlsperger, "The FPÖ and the Right," in *Contemporary Austrian Studies*, v. 4: *Austro-Corporatism – Part, Present, Future*, ed. Günther Bischof and Anton Pelinka (New Brunswick, NJ: Transaction, 1996), p. 354.

46 Lothar Höbelt, *Von der Vierten Partei zur Dritten Kraft: Die Geschichte des VdU* (Graz: Stocker, 1999), pp. 75–76, 90.

47 Maj. J. V. Milano, Memorandum for the Record, September 26, 1949, NARA, RG 319, IRR Spider, XA 000902.

48 On his wartime role see Radomir V. Luza, *Resistance in Austria, 1938-1945* (Minneapolis: University of Minnesota Press, 1984), p. 168. On his expectations see Appendix A to Special Agents F. K. Richter, Carl H. Kock, and Frank P. Otto, Memorandum for the Officer in Charge, The League of Independents, Report No. 2, September 13, 1949, NARA, RG 319, IRR Spider, XA 000902.

49 Appendix C to Special Agents F. K. Richter, Carl H. Kock, and Frank P. Otto, Memorandum for the Officer in Charge, The League of Independents, Report No. 2, September 13, 1949, NARA, RG 319, IRR Spider, XA 000902. See also Appendix G of that document for an assessment of Schwarzkopf.

50 Donald Robert Whitnah and Florentine E. Whitnah, *Salzburg Under Siege: US Occupation, 1945–1955* (New York: Greenwood, 1991). Siegfried Beer, "Hunting the Discriminators: Denazification in Austria, 1945–1947," in *Racial Discrimination and Ethnicity in European History*, ed., Guômundur Hálfdanarson (Pisa: PLUS, 2003), pp. 177–92.

51 Appendix G of Special Agents F. K. Richter, Carl H. Kock, and Frank P. Otto, Memorandum for the Officer in Charge, The League of Independents, Report No. 2, September 13, 1949, NARA, RG 319, IRR Spider, XA 000902.

52 Memorandum for the Officer in Charge, September 30, 1949, NARA, RG 319, IRR Spider, XA 000902. See also Special Agents F. K. Richter, Carl H. Kock, and Frank P. Otto, Memorandum for the Officer in Charge, The League of Independents, Report No. 2, September 13, 1949, NARA, RG 319, IRR Spider, XA 000902.

53 Appendix "J": Life History of Erich Kernmayer, born 27 February 1906 in Land Graz, Styria, NARA, RG 319, IRR Spider, XA 000902.

54 Appendix G to Special Agents F. K. Richter, Carl H. Kock, and Frank P. Otto, Memorandum for the Officer in Charge, The League of Independents, Report No. 2, September 13, 1949, NARA, RG 319, IRR Spider, XA 000902.

55 Breitman, et. al., *U.S. Intelligence and the Nazis*, p. 276.

56 Appendix G to Special Agents F. K. Richter, Carl H. Kock, and Frank P. Otto, Memorandum for the Officer in Charge, The League of Independents, Report No. 2, September 13, 1949, NARA, RG 319, IRR Spider, XA 000902.

57 Special Agents Carl H. Koch, F. K. Richter, and Frank P. Otto, Memorandum for the Officer In Charge, CIC Salzburg, Ref. No. S-5560, September 28, 1949, NARA, RG 319, IRR Spider, XA 000902. On sales see Kernmayer's intercepted letter of August 21 1951, NARA, RG 319, IRR Erich Kernmayer, XE 189259. On the banning of the book see NARA, RG 319, IRR Grosse Rauch, MSN 50254.

58 AG 383.7, December 16, 1948; John B. Burkel (Chief, CIC Land Salzburg Sub-Detachment, June 8, 1949; Berg MSG No. 1-X, Salzburg to Linz, December 27, 1948; and Untitled Security Information memo dated July 3, 1952, all in NARA, RG 319, IRR Kernmayer, Erich, XE 189259.

59 Appendix C of Special Agents F. K. Richter, Carl H. Kock, and Frank P. Otto, Memorandum for the Officer in Charge, The League of Independents, Report No. 2, September 13, 1949, NARA, RG 319, IRR Spider, XA 000902.

60 Appendix H to Special Agents F. K. Richter, Carl H. Kock, and Frank P. Otto, Memorandum for the Officer in Charge, The League of Independents, Report No. 2, September 13, 1949, NARA, RG 319, IRR Spider, XA 000902.

61 Special Agents F. K. Richter, Carl H. Kock, and Frank P. Otto, Memorandum for the Officer in Charge, The League of Independents, Report No. 2, September 13, 1949, NARA, RG 319, IRR Spider, XA 000902.

62 Appendix D to Special Agents F. K. Richter, Carl H. Kock, and Frank P. Otto, Memorandum for the Officer in Charge, The League of Independents, Report No. 2, September 13, 1949, NARA, RG 319, IRR Spider, XA 000902.

63 Appendix C of Special Agents F. K. Richter, Carl H. Kock, and Frank P. Otto, Memorandum for the Officer in Charge, The League of Independents, Report No. 2, September 13, 1949, NARA, RG 319, IRR Spider, XA 000902.

64 Special Agents F. K. Richter, Carl H. Kock, and Frank P. Otto, Memorandum for the Officer in Charge, The League of Independents, Report No. 2, September 13, 1949, NARA, RG 319, IRR Spider, XA 000902.

65 Special Agents F. K. Richter, Carl H. Kock, and Frank P. Otto, Memorandum for the Officer in Charge, The League of Independents, Report No. 2, September 13, 1949, NARA, RG 319, IRR Spider, XA 000902. Also Appendix C of that document.

66 Memorandum for the Officer in Charge, September 30, 1949, NARA, RG 319, IRR Spider, XA 000902.

67 Höbelt, *Geschichte des VdU*, p. 70.

68 Appendix E to Special Agents F. K. Richter, Carl H. Kock, and Frank P. Otto, Memorandum for the Officer in Charge, The League of Independents, Report No. 2, September 13, 1949, NARA, RG 319, IRR Spider, XA 000902.

69 Memorandum for the Officer in Charge, September 30, 1949, NARA, RG 319, Entry, IRR Spider, XA 000902. See also James A Reeder, Branch Chief, Political and Economic Branch, to Chief of Operations, 430th CIC Detachment, United States Forces Austria, September 30, 1949, NARA, RG 319, IRR Spider, XA 000902.

70 Lankford Informal Memorandum to Colonel Schrantz, September 20, 1949, NARA, RG 319, IRR Spider, XA 000902.

71 Appendix C to Special Agents F. K. Richter, Carl H. Kock, and Frank P. Otto, Memorandum for the Officer in Charge, The League of Independents, Report No. 2, September 13, 1949, NARA, RG 319, IRR Spider, XA 000902.

72 Appendix A to Special Agents F. K. Richter, Carl H. Kock, and Frank P. Otto, Memorandum for the Officer in Charge, The League of Independents, Report No. 2, September 13, 1949, NARA, RG 319, IRR Spider, XA 000902.

73 Civil Censorship Group Austria, Recorded Telephone Conversation between Kraus and Rohrbacher, September 27, 1949, NARA, RG 319, IRR Spider, XA 000902.

74 Maj. J. V. Milano, Memo for the Record, August 10, 1949, NARA, RG 319, Entry, IRR Spider, XA 000902. Also Maj. J. V. Milano, Memorandum for the Record, September 26, 1949, NARA, RG 319, IRR Spider, XA 000902.

75 Peter Sonnenberg, "Medienkontrolle während der NS-Zeit: Eine kollektiv-biographische Analyse ausgewählter Journalisten der 1938 verbotenen Wiener Tageszeitungen "Wiener Tag" und "Telegraf." Magisterarbeit, Universität Wien, 2009, p. 51.

76 Robert S. Seaver, Chief, CIC Land Salzburg Sub-Detachment, CIC Salzburg Ref. No. S-5471, Memorandum for the Officer in Charge, September 16, 1949, NARA, RG 319, IRR Spider, XA 000902.

77 For his activities see NARA, RG 319, IRR Kernmayer, Erich, XE 189259.

78 Col. Hugh H. Sargent, HQ, 430th CIC Detachment, September 9, 1952, and Biographic Report A-49, Kraus, Herbert, May 12, 1953, NARA, RG 319, IRR Kraus, Herbert, XA 010790; Secret Report on the Bruderschaft, Enclosure to HICOG Frankfurt 969, June 7, 1950, NARA, RG 319, IRR Die Bruderschaft v. 1, D 267740.

CENTRAL INTELLIGENCE AGENCY

WASHINGTON 25, D.C.

OFFICE OF THE DIRECTOR

5 MAY 1952

Mr. Argyle R. Mackey
Commissioner of Immigration
and Naturalization
Department of Justice
Washington 25, D.C.

SUBJECT: Mykola LEBED

Dear Sir:

... invaluable value to this Agency in its operations. In connection
with future Agency operations of the first importance, it is
urgently necessary that subject be able to travel in Western
Europe. Before subject undertakes such travel, however, this
Agency must be in a position to assure his reentry into the United
States without investigation or incident which would attract undue
attention to his activities. Your Service has indicated that it
cannot give such assurance because of the fact that subject was
convicted in 1936 of complicity in the 1934 assassination of the
Polish Minister of the Interior and sentenced to death, later
commuted to life imprisonment. Subject's trial by the Polish
court was largely influenced by political factors and this Agency
has no reason to disbelieve subject's denial of complicity in this
assassination. However, the conviction of a crime involving moral
turpitude raises the question of subject's admissibility to the
United States under the Immigration laws. Your Service has indicated that, if the subject reenters the United States on a reentry
permit, an investigation must then be conducted. Such investiga-

In order to remove the obstacles to the fulfillment of this
Agency's projected operations and pursuant to the authority granted
under Section 8 of the CIA Act of 1949, I approve and recommend for
your approval, the entrance of this subject into the United States
for permanent residence under the above Act because such entry is
essential to the furtherance of the national intelligence mission
and is in the interest of national security. In accordance with
previous correspondence in Section 8 cases, it is understood that
you will present this matter to the Attorney General for his
approval. There is attached a memorandum of biographical information and Form I-135 in duplicate.

In line with the suggestion made in your letter of 21 March
1952, it will be appreciated if you will record the subject's
admission for permanent residence as of the date of his original
entry, 4 October 1949, to coincide with date of entry of his
wife and daughter.

In view of the urgency in this case, it would be appreciated
if you would give it your expeditious consideration.

Sincerely,

Allen W. Dulles
Deputy Director

The CIA moved to protect Ukranian nationalist leader Mykola Lebed from criminal investigation by the
Immigration and Naturalization Service in 1952. *RG 263, Records of the Central Intelligence Agency.*

CHAPTER FIVE

Collaborators: Allied Intelligence and the

Organization of Ukrainian Nationalists

Newly released Army and CIA records have many thousands of pages on Nazi collaborators during and after World War II. The records are especially rich concerning Allied relationships with Ukrainian nationalist organizations after 1945. This section focuses on the Organization of Ukrainian Nationalists under Stephen Bandera and the exile representation of the Ukrainian underground government (ZP/UHVR), which was dominated by Bandera's one-time followers-turned-rivals, including Mykola Lebed. The level of detail in the new records allows a fuller and more accurate picture of their relationships with Allied intelligence over several decades.[1]

Background

The Organization of Ukrainian Nationalists (OUN), founded in 1929 by western Ukrainians from East Galicia, called for an independent and ethnically homogenous Ukraine. Its prime enemy was Poland, which then controlled the ethnically mixed regions of East Galicia and Volhynia. The OUN assassinated Polish Interior Minister Bronislaw Pieracki in 1934. Among those tried, convicted, and imprisoned for the murder in 1936 were young OUN activists Stephan Bandera and Mykola Lebed. The court sentenced them to death, and the state commuted the sentences to life imprisonment.[2] The convicted Ukrainians escaped when the Germans invaded Poland in 1939.

After the Nazi-Soviet Pact of 1939 awarded Eastern Galicia and Volhynia to the USSR, the OUN turned its hopes toward the Germans. In late 1939 the Germans housed OUN leaders in Krakow, then the capital of the German-occupied General Government. In 1940 the OUN split over political strategy. The older wing under Andrei Melnik (OUN/M) aimed to work closely with the Germans while waiting patiently for Ukraine's independence. Bandera's wing (OUN/B) was a militant fascist organization that wanted Ukrainian independence immediately.

After the Germans invaded the USSR on June 22, 1941, Bandera's teams moved into East Galicia. On reaching the East Galician capital city of Lwów on June 30, 1941, his closest deputy Jaroslav Stetsko proclaimed a "sovereign and united" Ukrainian state in the name of Bandera and the OUN/B. Stetsko was to be the new prime minister and Lebed, having trained at a Gestapo center in Zakopane, the new minister for security.[3]

Determined to exploit Ukraine for themselves, the Germans insisted that Bandera and Stetsko rescind this proclamation. When they refused, they, along with other OUN/B leaders, were arrested. Bandera and Stetsko were held initially in Berlin under house arrest. After January 1942 they were sent to Sachsenhausen concentration camp but in comparatively comfortable confinement. Administrative and senior auxiliary police positions in western Ukraine went to Melnik's group.[4] German security police formations, meanwhile, were ordered to arrest and kill Bandera loyalists in western Ukraine for fear that they would rise against German rule.[5]

After Lebed escaped, he assumed control of the OUN/B in western Ukraine, which now operated underground. Eventually the OUN/B dominated the Ukrainian Insurgent Army (UPA), a guerrilla force originally formed in 1942 to engage all political and ethnic enemies including Germans and Soviets. Eastern Ukrainians later claimed that the Bandera's group took over the UPA by assassinating the original leaders.[6] By 1944 the terms "UPA" and "Baderovsty" became interchangeable, though not all UPA fighters came from the OUN/B. The OUN/B relationship with the Germans in western Ukraine was complicated. On the one hand, it fought German rule, and the Gestapo put a price on Lebed's head. On the other, it pursued its own ethnic cleansing policies complementing German aims.

A Banderist proclamation in April 1941 claimed that "Jews in the USSR constitute the most faithful support of the ruling Bolshevik regime and the vanguard of Muscovite imperialism in the Ukraine."[7] Stetsko, even while under house arrest in July 1941, said that "I…fully appreciate the undeniably harmful and hostile role of the Jews, who are helping Moscow to enslave Ukraine…. I therefore support the destruction of the Jews and the expedience of bringing German methods of exterminating Jewry to Ukraine…."[8] In Lwów, a leaflet warned Jews that, "You welcomed Stalin with flowers [when the Soviets occupied East Galicia in 1939]. We will lay your heads at Hitler's feet."[9] At a July 6, 1941, meeting in Lwów, Bandera loyalists determined that Jews "have to be treated harshly…. We must finish them off…. Regarding the Jews, we will adopt any methods that lead to their destruction."[10] Indeed pogroms in East Galicia in the war's first days killed perhaps 12,000 Jews.[11] Back in Berlin, Stetsko reported it all to Bandera.[12]

Nazi authorities mobilized Ukrainians into auxiliary police units, some of which cleared ghettos. Few such auxiliary police belonged to Bandera's group, which operated independently. But Banderist guerrillas in western Ukraine often killed Jews. Historian Yehuda Bauer writes that Banderists "killed all the Jews they could find," surely "many thousands" in all.[13] Moshe Maltz, a Jew living in hiding in Sokal, heard from a friendly Polish contact "about 40 Jews who were hiding out in the woods near his home … the Bandera gangs came and murdered them all."[14]

When the Soviets reconquered East Galicia in November 1944, there were few Jews there left alive. But Maltz recorded that, "When the Bandera gangs seize a Jew, they consider it a prize catch. The ordinary Ukrainians feel the same way…. they all want to participate in the heroic act of killing a Jew. They literally slash Jews to pieces with their machetes…."[15]

When the war turned against the Germans in early 1943, leaders of Bandera's group believed that the Soviets and Germans would exhaust each other, leaving an independent Ukraine as in 1918. Lebed proposed in April to "cleanse the entire revolutionary territory of the Polish population," so that a resurgent Polish state would not claim the region as in 1918.[16] Ukrainians serving as auxiliary policemen for the Germans now joined the Ukrainian Insurgent Army (UPA). Maltz recorded that "Bandera men … are not discriminating about who they kill; they are gunning down the populations of entire villages…. Since there are hardly any Jews left to kill, the Bandera gangs have turned on the Poles. They are literally hacking Poles to pieces. Every day ... you can see the bodies of Poles, with wires around their necks, floating down the river Bug."[17] On a single day, July 11, 1943, the UPA attacked some 80 localities killing perhaps 10,000 Poles.[18]

As the Red Army moved into western Ukraine (it liberated Lwów in July 1944) the UPA resisted the Soviet advance with full-scale guerrilla war. Maltz noted that, "Most of the Bandera gangs, men and women, from the villages ... are still hiding out in the woods, armed to the teeth, and hold up Soviet soldiers. The Soviets may be the rulers of the towns, but the Bandera gangs reign supreme in the surrounding countryside, especially at night. The Russians...have their hands full.... Hardly a day passes without a Soviet official being killed...."[19] The Banderists and UPA also resumed cooperation with the Germans. Though the SD was pleased with the intelligence received from the UPA on the Soviets, the Wehrmacht viewed Banderist terror against Polish civilians as counterproductive.[20]

In July 1944 nationalists in Ukraine formed the Supreme Ukrainian Liberation Council (UHVR), which served as an underground Ukrainian government in the Carpathian mountains. The UPA, now operating against the Soviets in smaller groups, was its army. The dominant political party in the UHVR was the Bandera group.[21] In September 1944 the Germans released Bandera and Stetsko from Sachsenhausen. Berlin hoped to form a Ukrainian National Committee with both OUN factions and other Ukrainian leaders. The Committee was formed in November, but Bandera and Stetsko refused to cooperate. They escaped from Berlin in December and fled south, emerging after the war in Munich.[22]

By 1947 some 250,000 Ukrainians were living as displaced persons in Germany, Austria, and Italy, many of them OUN activists or sympathizers.[23] After 1947 UPA fighters began crossing into the U.S. zone, having reached the border on foot through Czechoslovakia. They tended to be Banderist in their sympathies. We cannot describe here the background of most UPA men who reached the U.S. zone.[24] But Mykola Ninowskyj's story, which comes from a 1956 West German arrest report obtained by the CIA, may be typical. Born in 1920, Ninowskyj joined one of the Ukrainian battalions that advanced into East Galicia under German command in 1941. Later in the year he joined the 201st Schutzmannschaft (Auxiliary Police) Battalion, which conducted what he described as "anti-partisan" operations in Belorussia. Under German direction, many of these battalions murdered Jews. In 1944 he returned to Galicia as a Banderist guerrilla fighter until 1948 when he made his way west as a courier. "I am on the Bandera side," he told police in 1956.[25]

In the early postwar years Ukrainian DP camps were hotbeds of nationalist proselytizing. Bandera was determined to assert control over the émigré community. In February 1946 he formed the Foreign Section OUN (ZCh/OUN), an exile branch of the Bandera group, in which he maintained "a firm line on all questions, political education, ideological and political unity, and discipline of the membership."[26] Bandera intended to create a dictatorship in exile, which he would then transfer to a liberated Ukraine. According to U.S. Army CIC observers, the Foreign Section OUN routinely used intimidation and even terror against political enemies. CIC reports listed Bandera as "extremely dangerous" because he was willing to use violence against Ukrainian rivals in Germany.[27]

In July 1944, before the Soviets took Lwów, the UHVR sent a delegation of its senior officials to establish contact with the Vatican and Western governments. The delegation was known as the Foreign Representation of the Supreme Ukrainian Liberation Council (ZP/UHVR). It included Father Ivan Hrinioch as president of the ZP/UHVR; Mykola Lebed as its Foreign Minister; and Yuri Lopatinski as the UPA delegate. Hrinioch was a Ukrainian Catholic priest and nationalist, who was in Krakow with Bandera and Lebed in 1940. He served as liaison between Archbishop Andrei Shepstitski of Lwów and Bishop Ivan Buczko, the Uniate Church's representative at the Vatican. When the Germans invaded East Galicia, Hrinioch also had a relationship with Fritz Arlt, a "Jewish expert" in the SD, who worked under General Governor Hans Frank in 1940 and was charged with contacting Soviet émigrés to serve as German-allied volunteers during the invasion in 1941.[28] Until 1948, all three envoys were members of the OUN/B party and loyal to Bandera.

In its initial manifesto of July 1944, the UHVR had called for unity of "all leading political elements, irrespective of their ideological convictions or political affiliation, who uphold the political sovereignty of the Ukrainian state [and] a popular democratic mode of determining the political system...."[29] If nothing else, western Ukrainians learned during the war that they would have to appeal to eastern Ukrainians, from whom they had been separated by geography and religion for centuries. The UHVR later rejected "attempts by western Ukrainian chauvinists, including Stephen Bandera, to erect a Ukrainian state on a narrowly religious, mono-party, totalitarian basis, since the Eastern Ukrainian nationalists find such a political philosophy unacceptable."[30]

A feud erupted in 1947 between Bandera and Stetsko on the one hand, and Hrinioch and Lebed on the other. Bandera and Stetsko insisted on an independent Ukraine under a single party led by one man, Bandera. Hrynioch and Lebed declared that the people in the homeland, not Bandera, created the UHVR, and that they would never accept Bandera as dictator.

At an August 1948 Congress of the OUN Foreign Section, Bandera expelled the Hrinioch-Lebed group from the party and ordered his own followers in their organization to resign. Bandera still controlled 80 percent of the party and claimed exclusive authority to direct the Ukrainian national movement at home and in the emigration. He also continued terror tactics against anti-Banderist Ukrainian leaders in Western Europe and maneuvered for control of Ukrainian émigré organizations. U.S. intelligence officials estimated that up to 80 percent of all Ukrainian DPs from Eastern Galicia were loyal to Bandera. But Lebed, Hrinioch, and Lopatinky remained the official UHVR representation abroad.[31]

By this time, the split was no longer just an issue for Ukrainian émigrés. Owing to the Berlin Blockade, the Cold War between the western Allies and the USSR threatened to erupt into fighting, and Allied intelligence organizations, which were interested in Ukrainian contacts, had to choose sides.

Allied Intelligence and Stephen Bandera

The CIC first became interested in Stephen Bandera in September 1945. As UPA guerrillas made their way by foot into the U.S. Zone of Germany, the CIC interrogated them as to the military situation in western Ukraine, the makeup of UPA units, their contacts in the U.S. zone, and their connection with Bandera himself.[32] In 1947 the flow of UPA fighters increased owing to Operation Vistula, a Polish army effort to destroy the UPA in southeastern Poland, and more information became available.

The guerrillas said that most UPA fighters were "ordinary" Banderists, but others also listed Slovak Hlinka Guards, Ukrainian SS from the 14th Grenadier Waffen-SS (Galicia) Division, and "escaped German SS men" as those among the UPA forces. Most UPA fighters recognized Bandera as their leader.[33] UPA refugees also viewed themselves as refitting rather than quitting. One source said in September 1947 that Banderists were recruiting more members in DP camps, their main recruiter being Anton Eichner, a former SS officer.[34] Other interrogations revealed that, "the UPA foresees an end to communism within the very near future… Once the war comes… they hope to… fight either as front shock troops or gain in their old capacity, as guerilla fighters behind the Russian lines…."[35]

By August 1947 Banderists were represented in every Ukrainian DP camp in the U.S. zone as well as in the British and French zones. They had a sophisticated courier system reaching into the Ukraine. The CIC termed Bandera himself, then in Munich, as "extremely dangerous." He was "constantly en route, frequently in disguise," with bodyguards ready to "do away with any person who may be dangerous to [Bandera] or his party." UPA fighters said that Bandera was "looked upon as the spiritual and national hero of all Ukrainians…."[36]

Banderists represented themselves as fighting a "heroic Ukrainian resistance against the Nazis and the Communists" which had been "misrepresented and maligned" by "Moscow propaganda." Bandera, they never tired of saying, had been arrested by the Nazis and held in Sachsenhausen. Now he and his movement fought "not only for the Ukraine, but also for all of Europe."[37] As for Banderist activities before and during the war, U.S. intelligence officials seemed to understand little beyond Bandera's implication in the Pierecki assassination. They understood nothing of the Banderist role in ethnic cleansing during the war.

CIC agents also used UPA informants to ferret out Soviet spies from Ukrainian DP camps who slipped into Germany with UPA partisans. The Soviets had penetrated the UPA bands that made their way west.[38] Yuri Lopatinski travelled to the Ukrainian camp in Deggendorf in October 1947 to find Soviet agents.[39] UPA members could also provide intelligence on the Soviets since, according to UPA officers, they had "done a fairly thorough job of penetrating MVD and Polish intelligence units."[40] "Don't you think," said one CIC memo, "that this is a H[ell] of a good opportunity to recruit some high class informants?"[41]

In November 1947 the Soviet military authorities in Berlin insisted that UPA members in the U.S. zone be handed over. "Almost all of them, said Lt. Col. Igor Bantsyrev (the Chief Soviet Repatriation Representative), "are Soviet citizens who participated in the war … against the Allied nations on the side of the German fascist Army."[42] CIC officers recommended against it. Extradition of the UPA partisans, said one, could "destroy for years the confidence all anti-Bolshevist forces have in the USA."[43]

The Soviets learned that Bandera was in the U.S. zone and demanded his arrest. A covert Soviet team even entered the U.S. zone in June 1946 to kidnap Bandera.[44] The Strategic Services Unit, the postwar successor to the OSS and predecessor to the CIA, did not know about the Soviet team. Nonetheless, they feared the "serious effects on Soviet-American relations likely to ensue from open US connivance in the unhampered continuance of [Bandera's] anti-Soviet activities on German soil."[45] Since Bandera himself was not trustworthy, they were just as pleased to get rid of him.

Despite "an extensive and aggressive search" in mid-1947 that included regular weekly updates, CIC officials could not locate Bandera.[46] Few photos of him existed. One CIC agent complained that Bandera's agents in Germany "have been instructed to disseminate false information concerning the personal description of Bandera."[47] Bandera's agents misled CIC as to his location as well. "Aware of our desire to locate Bandera," read one report, "[they] deliberately attempt to 'throw us off the track' by giving out false leads."[48] CIC suspended the search. Zsolt Aradi, a Hungarian-born journalist with high Vatican contacts and the chief contact at the Vatican for the Strategic Services Unit (SSU), warned that Bandera's handover to the Soviets would destroy any relationship with the UHVR, which at the time was headed by Banderist members, and with Ukrainian clerics at the Vatican like Buczko, who were sympathetic to Bandera.[49]

The CIA never considered entering into an alliance with Bandera to procure intelligence from Ukraine. "By nature," read a CIA report, "[Bandera] is a political intransigent of great personal ambition, who [has] since April 1948, opposed all political organizations in the emigration which favor a representative form of government in the Ukraine as opposed to a mono-party, OUN/Bandera regime." Worse, his intelligence operatives in Germany were dishonest and not secure.[50] Debriefings of couriers from western Ukraine in 1948 confirmed that, "the thinking of Stephan Bandera and his immediate émigré supporters [has] become radically outmoded in the Ukraine." Bandera was also a convicted assassin. By now, word had reached the CIA of Bandera's fratricidal struggles with other Ukrainian groups during the war and in the emigration. By 1951 Bandera turned vocally anti-American as well, since the US did not advocate an independent Ukraine."[51] The CIA had an agent within the Bandera group in 1951 mostly to keep an eye on Bandera.[52]

British Intelligence (MI6), however, was interested in Bandera. MI6 first contacted Bandera through Gerhard von Mende in April 1948. An ethnic German from Riga, von Mende served in Alfred Rosenberg's Ostministerium during the war as head of the section for the Caucasus and Turkestan section, recruiting Soviet Muslims from central Asia for use against the USSR. In this capacity he was kept personally informed of UPA actions and capabilities.[53] Nothing came of initial British contacts with Bandera because, as the CIA learned later, "the political, financial, and tech requirements of the [Ukrainians] were higher than the British cared to meet." But by 1949 MI6 began helping Bandera send his own agents into western Ukraine via airdrop. In 1950 MI6 began training these agents on the expectation that they could provide intelligence from western Ukraine.[54]

CIA and State Department officials flatly opposed the use of Bandera. By 1950 the CIA was working with the Hrinioch-Lebed group, and had begun to run its own agents into western Ukraine to make contact with the UHVR. Bandera no longer had the UHVR's support or even that of the OUN party leadership in Ukraine. Bandera's agents also deliberately worked against Ukrainian agents used by the CIA. In April 1951 CIA officials tried to convince MI6 to pull support from Bandera. MI6 refused. They thought that Bandera could run his agents without British support, and MI6 were "seeking progressively to assume control of Bandera's lines."[55] The British also thought that the CIA underestimated Bandera's importance. "Bandera's name," they said, "still carried considerable weight in the Ukraine and ... the UPA would look to him first and foremost."[56]

Moreover, MI6 argued, Bandera's group was "the strongest Ukrainian organization abroad, is deemed competent to train party cadres, [and] build a morally and politically healthy organization...."[57]

British officials considered "the possibility and desirability of engaging in clandestine operations in the Soviet Union other than those of a purely intelligence-gathering character."[58] But the CIA and State Department officials were "very strongly opposed" to London's idea of returning Bandera to the Ukraine. Bandera, the Americans said, had "lost touch with feelings in the Ukraine, particularly in the former Polish territories where... the Soviet government had been successful to a remarkable degree in transforming the mentality of the younger generation."[59] For the CIA, the best solution for intelligence in the Ukraine was the "political neutralization of Bandera as an individual...."[60] The British argued that such "would lead to a drying up of recruits" and "would disrupt British operations...."[61] MI6 disregarded the CIA statement that "Bandera...is politically unacceptable to the US Government."

British operations through Bandera expanded. An early 1954 MI6 summary noted that, "the operational aspect of this [British] collaboration [with Bandera] was developing satisfactorily. Gradually a more complete control was obtained over infiltration operations and although the intelligence dividend was low it was considered worthwhile to proceed...."[62] Bandera was, according to his handlers, "a professional underground worker with a terrorist background and ruthless notions about the rules of the game.... A bandit type if you like, with a burning patriotism, which provides an ethical background and a justification for his banditry. No better and no worse than others of his kind...."[63]

From inside the Ukraine, the UHVR rejected Bandera's authoritarian approach and demanded unity in the emigration. In messages brought from the Ukraine by CIA agents, UHVR insisted in the summer of 1953 that Lebed represented "the entire Ukrainian liberation movement in the homeland."[64] American and British officials tried to reconcile Bandera to Lebed's leadership, but Bandera and Stetsko refused. In February 1954 London had enough. "There appeared," reported Bandera's handlers, "to be no alternative but to break with Bandera in order to safeguard the healthy ZCh/OUN elements remaining and be able to continue using them operationally.... The break between us was complete." MI6 dropped all agents-in-training still loyal to Bandera.[65] In July MI6 informed Lebed that it "would not resume [its] relationship with Bandera under any circumstances." MI6 maintained its four wireless links in Ukraine, now run by a reconstituted ZCh/OUN, and shared intelligence from the links with Lebed and the CIA.[66] The degree to which MI6's links into Ukraine were compromised all along owing to the insecurity of Bandera's lines is not clear.[67]

Bandera remained in Munich. He had two British-trained radio operators, and he continued to recruit agents on his own. He published a newspaper that spewed anti-American rhetoric and used loyal thugs to attack other Ukrainian émigré newspapers and to terrorize political opponents in the Ukrainian emigration. He attempted to penetrate U.S. military and intelligence offices in Europe and to intimidate Ukrainians working for the United States. He continued to run agents into the Ukraine, financing them with counterfeit U.S. money. By 1957 the CIA and MI6 concluded that all former Bandera agents in Ukraine were under Soviet control.[68] The question was what to do. U.S. and British intelligence officials lamented that "despite our unanimous desire to 'quiet' Bandera, precautions must be taken to see that the Soviets are not allowed to kidnap or kill him ... under no circumstances must Bandera be allowed to become a martyr."[69]

Meanwhile, Bandera searched for new sponsors. For a brief time in early 1956, Italian Military Intelligence (SIFAR) sponsored him, surely not understanding that his lines were compromised.[70] The BND, the West German intelligence service under former Wehrmacht Gen. Reinhard Gehlen, formed a new relationship with Bandera. It was a natural union. During the war, Gehlen's senior officers argued that the USSR could be broken up if only Germany wooed the various nationalities properly. Bandera had continued lines into the Ukraine, and in March 1956 he offered these in return for money and weapons.[71] The CIA warned the West Germans that "against any [operative] relationship with Bandera," noting that, "we [are] convinced [that] all alleged Bandera assets in CSR, Poland, and Ukraine [are] non-existent or non-effective. We also note rapidity and thoroughness of [Soviet] rollups [of] his past ops indicate weak OUN/B security."[72]

The Bavarian state government and Munich police wanted to crack down on Bandera's organization for crimes ranging from counterfeiting to kidnapping. Von Mende, now a West German government official, protected him. Bandera gave von Mende political reports, which von Mende relayed to the West German

Foreign Office. Von Mende routinely intervened with the Bavarian government on Bandera's behalf for residency permits and the like, and now intervened with the Bavarian authorities for "false passports and other documentation."[73] The exact results of von Mende's help are not clear, but Bandera was left alone.

In April 1959 Bandera again asked West German intelligence for support and this time Gehlen was interested. The CIA noted that, "It [is] apparent that Bandera [is] seeking support for illegal ops into Ukraine." The West Germans agreed to support at least one such mission based on the "fact [that] Bandera and group no longer the cut throats they were" and because Bandera "supplied proof [of] existing contact with inside assets." A team trained and funded by the BND crossed from Czechoslovakia in late July, and the BND promised Bandera support for future operations if this one were to be even "moderately successful."[74]

Bandera's personal contact in West German intelligence was Heinz Danko Herre, Gehlen's old deputy in Fremde Heere Ost who had worked with the Gen. Andrei Vlassov's army of Russian émigrés and former prisoners in the last days of the war and was now Gehlen's closest adviser.[75] CIA officials in Munich repeated the usual warnings. Herre was not dissuaded. "Bandera," Herre said, "has been known to us for about 20 years [!].... Within and without Germany he has over half a million followers." Herre, reported the CIA base in Munich is aware of Bandera's earlier reputation [but] is aware that nothing has happened, during the period of [BND's] association, indicating that Bandera still is using his earlier rough tactics.... [Herre] also feels that, in principle, Bandera has more to offer operationally than most if not all other Russian (sic) émigré groups in the West today.[76]

Herre admitted that West German use of Bandera was a "closely held" secret even within the BND and that the relationship was "not cleared with Bonn due to political overtones."[77] By September Herre reported that the BND was getting "good [foreign intelligence] reports on the Soviet Ukraine" as a result of their operations.[78] He offered to keep CIA fully informed as to Bandera's activities in return for a favor. Bandera had been trying to obtain a U.S. visa since 1955 in order to meet with Ukrainian supporters in the United States and to meet with State Department and CIA officials. Herre thought that a visa procured with West German help would improve his own relationship with Bandera. CIA officials in Munich actually recommended the visa in October 1959.[79]

But on October 15, 1959, only 10 days after the CIA Munich base made the request, a KGB assassin named Bogdan Stashinskiy murdered Bandera with a special gun that sprayed cyanide dust into the victim's face. The Soviets, who had penetrated Bandera's organization and the BND years before, evidently decided that they could not live with another alliance between German intelligence officers and Ukrainian fanatics. Stashinskiy received the Order of the Red Banner for the job.[80]

U.S. Consul General in Munich Edward Page noted that "assassinations are nothing new in the Ukrainian nationalist movement." Though Bandera's death was demoralizing in the sense that the Soviets managed it under the noses of Bandera's bodyguards, Page noted that "many émigré figures do not personally lament his passing," given Bandera's strong-arm tactics with his political rivals in the Ukrainian emigration, particularly those leaning toward democratic institutions.[81] Bandera's faction continued to exist but was thoroughly penetrated by the KGB even at the highest levels.[82] Regardless, Herre maintained contact with Bandera's deputies in West Germany until 1961.[83]

The United States and Mykola Lebed

Mykola Lebed's relationship with the CIA lasted the entire length of the Cold War. While most CIA operations involving wartime perpetrators backfired, Lebed's operations augmented the fundamental instability of the Soviet Union.

Attempts to build a relationship in 1945 and 1946 between the SSU and the Hrinioch-Lebed group never materialized owing to its initial mistrust.[84] In December 1946 Hrinioch and Lopatinsky asked for U.S. help for operations in the Ukraine ranging from communications to agent training to money and weapons. In return, they would create intelligence networks in the Ukraine. Zsolt Aradi, the SSU's contact in the Vatican, approved the relationship. He noted that the "UHVR, UPA, and OUN-Bandera are the only large and efficient organizations among Ukrainians," and that Hrinioch, Lebed and Lopatinsky were "determined and able men… resolved to carry on…with or without us, and if necessary against us."[85] The SSU declined. A later report blamed the Ukrainians for "ineptitude in arguing their case and factionalism among the emigration."[86]

A CIC report from July 1947 cited sources that called Lebed a "well-known sadist and collaborator of the Germans."[87] Regardless, the CIC in Rome took up Lebed's offer whereby Lebed provided information on Ukrainian émigré groups, Soviet activities in the U.S. zone, and information on the Soviets and Ukrainians more generally. In Munich, Hrinioch became a CIC informant as well. In November 1947 Hrinioch requested on behalf of Bandera himself that the U.S. authorities move Lebed from Rome to Munich to protect him from Soviet extradition requests when American military government in Italy ended the following month. CIC in Munich was gaining Hrinioch's confidence and hoped to set up a meeting with Bandera himself.[88] The Army moved Lebed and his family to Munich in December. In the meantime, Lebed sanitized his wartime record and that of the Bandera group and UPA with a 126-page book on the latter which emphasized their fight against the Germans and Soviets.[89]

The Berlin Blockade in 1948 and the threat of a European war prompted the CIA to scrutinize Soviet émigré groups and the degree to which they could provide crucial intelligence. In Project ICON, the CIA studied 30 groups and recommended operational cooperation with the Hrinioch-Lebed group as the organization best suited for clandestine work. Compared with Bandera, Hrinioch and Lebed represented a moderate, stable, and operationally secure group with the firmest connections to the Ukrainian underground in the USSR. A resistance/intelligence group behind Soviet lines would be useful if war broke out. The CIA provided money, supplies, training, facilities for radio broadcasts, and parachute drops of trained agents to augment slower courier routes through Czechoslovakia used by UPA fighters and messengers.[90] As Lebed put it later, "the ... drop operations were the first real indication ... that American Intelligence was willing to give active support to establishing lines of communication into the Ukraine."[91]

CIA operations with these Ukrainians began in 1948 under the cryptonym CARTEL, soon changed to AERODYNAMIC. Hrinioch stayed in Munich, but Lebed relocated to New York and acquired permanent resident status, then U.S. citizenship. It kept him safe from assassination, allowed him to speak to Ukrainian émigré groups, and permitted him to return to the United States after operational trips to Europe. His identification in New York by other Ukrainians as a leader responsible for "wholesale murders of Ukrainians, Poles and Jewish (sic)," has been discussed elsewhere.[92]

Once in the United States, Lebed was the CIA's chief contact for AERODYNAMIC. CIA handlers pointed to his "cunning character," his "relations with the Gestapo and … Gestapo training," that the fact that he was "a very ruthless operator."[93] "Neither party," said one CIA official while comparing Bandera and Lebed, "is lily-white."[94] Like Bandera, Lebed was also constantly irritated that the United States never promoted the USSR's fragmentation along national lines; that the United States worked with imperial-minded Russian émigré groups as well as Ukrainian ones; and that the United States later followed a policy of peaceful coexistence with the Soviets.

On the other hand, Lebed had no personal political aspirations. He was unpopular among many Ukrainian émigrés owing to his brutal takeover of the UPA during the war—a takeover that included the assassination of rivals.[95] He was absolutely secure. To prevent Soviet penetration, he allowed no one in his inner circle who arrived in the West after 1945. He was said to have a first-rate operational mind, and by 1948 he was, according to Dulles, "of inestimable value to this Agency and its operations."[96] The CIA's AERODYNAMIC files contain tremendous operational detail on AERODYNAMIC, most of which cannot be recounted here.

AERODYNAMIC's first phase involved infiltration into Ukraine and then exfiltration of CIA-trained Ukrainian agents. By January 1950 the CIA's arm for the collection of secret intelligence (Office of Special Operations, OSO) and its arm for covert operations (Office of Policy Coordination, OPC) participated. Operations in that year revealed "a well established and secure underground movement" in the Ukraine that was even "larger and more fully developed than previous reports had indicated." Washington was especially pleased with the high level of UPA training in the Ukraine and its potential for further guerrilla actions, and with "the extraordinary news that … active resistance to the Soviet regime was spreading steadily eastward, out of the former Polish, Greek Catholic provinces."[97]

The CIA decided to expand its operations for "the support, development, and exploitation of the Ukrainian underground movement for resistance and intelligence purposes." "In view of the extent and activity of the resistance movement in the Ukraine," said OPC Chief Frank Wisner, "we consider this to be a top priority project."[98] The CIA learned of UPA activities in various Ukrainian districts; the Soviet commitment of police troops to destroy the UPA; the UPA's resonance with Ukrainians; and the UPA's potential to expand to 100,000 fighters in wartime. The work was not without hazards. Individual members of teams from 1949 to 1953 were captured and killed. By 1954 Lebed's group lost all contact with UHVR. By that time the Soviets subdued both the UHVR and UPA, and the CIA ended the aggressive phase of AERODYNAMIC.[99]

Beginning in 1953 AERODYNAMIC began to operate through a Ukrainian study group under Lebed's leadership in New York under CIA auspices, which collected Ukrainian literature and history and produced Ukrainian nationalist newspapers, bulletins, radio programming, and books for distribution in the Ukraine. In 1956 this group was formally incorporated as the non-profit Prolog Research and Publishing Association. It allowed the CIA to funnel funds as ostensible private donations without taxable footprints.[100] To avoid nosey New York State authorities, the CIA turned Prolog into a for-profit enterprise called Prolog Research Corporation, which ostensibly received private contracts. Under Hrinioch, Prolog maintained a Munich office named the Ukrainische-Gesellschaft für Auslandsstudien, EV. Most publications were created here.[101] The Hrinioch-Lebed organization still existed, but its activities ran entirely through Prolog.[102]

Prolog recruited and paid Ukrainian émigré writers who were generally unaware that they worked in a CIA-controlled operation. Only the six top members of the ZP/UHVR were witting agents. Beginning in 1955, leaflets were dropped over the Ukraine by air and radio broadcasts titled *Nova Ukraina* were aired in Athens for Ukrainian consumption. These activities gave way to systematic mailing campaigns to Ukraine through Ukrainian contacts in Poland and émigré contacts in Argentina, Australia, Canada, Spain, Sweden, and elsewhere. The newspaper *Suchasna Ukrainia* (Ukraine Today), *information bulletins,* a Ukrainian language journal for intellectuals called *Suchasnist* (The Present), and other publications were sent to libraries, cultural institutions, administrative offices and private individuals in Ukraine. These activities encouraged Ukrainian nationalism, strengthened Ukrainian resistance, and provided an alternative to Soviet media.[103]

In 1957 alone, with CIA support, Prolog broadcast 1,200 radio programs totaling 70 hours per month and distributed 200,000 newspapers and 5,000 pamphlets. In the years following, Prolog distributed books by nationalist

Ukrainian writers and poets. One CIA analyst judged that, "some form of nationalist feeling continues to exist [in the Ukraine] and … there is an obligation to support it as a cold war weapon." The distribution of literature in the Soviet Ukraine continued to the end of the Cold War.[104]

Prolog also garnered intelligence after Soviet travel restrictions eased somewhat in the late 1950s. It supported the travel of émigré Ukrainian students and scholars to academic conferences, international youth festivals, musical and dance performances, the Rome Olympics and the like, where they could speak with residents of the Soviet Ukraine in order to learn about living conditions there as well as the mood of Ukrainians toward the Soviet regime. Prolog's leaders and agents debriefed travelers on their return and shared information with the CIA. In 1966 alone Prolog personnel had contacts with 227 Soviet citizens. Beginning in 1960 Prolog also employed a CIA-trained Ukrainian spotter named Anatol Kaminsky. He created a net of informants in Europe and the United States made up of Ukrainian émigrés and other Europeans travelling to Ukraine who spoke with Soviet Ukrainians in the USSR or with Soviet Ukrainians travelling in the West. By 1966 Kaminsiky was Prolog's chief operations officer, while Lebed provided overall management.

In this guise, AERODYNAMIC was one of the most effective CIA operations in approaching disaffected Soviet citizens. In the 1960s Prolog's leaders provided reports on Ukrainian politics, dissident Ukrainian poets, individuals connected with the KGB as well as identities of KGB officers, Soviet missiles and aircraft in western Ukraine, and a host of other topics. Official Soviet attacks on the ZP/UHVR as Banderists, German collaborators, American agents, and the like were evidence of Prolog's effectiveness, as were Soviet crackdowns on Ukrainian writers and other dissidents in the mid to late 1960s. By that time Prolog influenced a new Ukrainian generation. By 1969 Ukrainians traveling from the USSR were instructed by dissidents there to take informational materials on Soviet repression in Ukraine only to ZP/UHVR personnel. Travelers to Ukraine even reported seeing ZP/UHVR literature in private homes. Prolog had become in the words of one senior CIA official, the sole "vehicle for CIA's operations directed at the Ukrainian Soviet Socialist Republic and [its] forty million Ukrainian citizens."[105]

Lebed overtly distanced himself and the Ukrainian national movement from the overt anti-Semitism of his Banderist days. In 1964 he publicly condemned in the name of the ZP/UHVR the appearance of *Judaism without Embellishment*, published by the Ukrainian Academy of Sciences in Kiev. The book was typical of the anti-Semitic diatribes of the early 20th century with the exception that it actually linked Jews with the Nazis in the attack on the USSR. The book signaled growing Soviet repression of dissident Jews, including the closing of synagogues and prohibitions on Passover Matzoh.[106] Lebed actually saw the book as a Soviet attempt to paint Ukrainians with a broad anti-Semitic brush. More to protect the name of Ukrainian nationalism, he publicly condemned the "provocative libel" and "slanderous statements" against Jews, adding in a particularly forgetful note that, "the Ukrainian people...are opposed to all and any preaching of hatred for other people."[107] Ironically, the CIA had Prolog translate sections of the book into French for distribution to left-wing groups in Europe who had been sympathetic to the Soviets. Former Banderists, in other words, now attacked the Soviets for anti-Semitism rather than with it.[108]

Lebed retired in 1975 but remained an adviser and consultant to Prolog and the ZP/UHVR. Roman Kupchinsky, a Ukrainian journalist who was a one-year-old when the war ended, became Prolog's chief in 1978. In the 1980s AERODYNAMIC's name was changed to QRDYNAMIC and in the 1980s PDDYNAMIC and then QRPLUMB. In 1977 President Carter's National Security Adviser Zbigniew Brzezinski helped to expand the program owing to what he called its "impressive dividends" and the "impact on specific audiences in the target area."[109] In the 1980s Prolog expanded its operations to reach other Soviet nationalities, and in a supreme irony, these included dissident Soviet Jews.[110] With the USSR teetering on the brink of collapse in 1990, QRPLUMB was terminated with a final payout of $1.75 million. Prolog could continue its activities, but it was on its own financially.[111]

In June 1985 the General Accounting Office mentioned Lebed's name in a public report on Nazis and collaborators who settled in the United States with help from U.S. intelligence agencies. The Office of Special Investigations (OSI) in the Department of Justice began investigating Lebed that year. The CIA worried that public scrutiny of Lebed would compromise QRPLUMB and that failure to protect Lebed would trigger outrage in the Ukrainian émigré community. It thus shielded Lebed by denying any connection between Lebed and the Nazis and by arguing that he was a Ukrainian freedom fighter. The truth, of course, was more complicated. As late as 1991 the CIA tried to dissuade OSI from approaching the German, Polish, and Soviet governments for war-related records related to the OUN. OSI eventually gave up the case, unable to procure definitive documents on Lebed. Mykola Lebed, Bandera's wartime chief in Ukraine, died in 1998. He is buried in New Jersey, and his papers are located at the Ukrainian Research Institute at Harvard University.

NOTES

1   On Allied relationships with the OUN/B see Stephen Dorril, *MI6*, pp. 222–48; Jeffrey Burds, *The Early Cold War in Soviet West Ukraine, 1944–1948*, Carl Beck Papers in Russian and East European Studies No. 1505 (Pittsburgh: Center for Russian and East European Studies, 2001). On cleavages in the Ukrainian emigration see Lubomyr Luciuk, *Searching for Place: Ukrainian Displaced Persons, Canada, and the Migration of Memory* (Toronto: University of Toronto Press, 2000); Vic Satzewich, *The Ukrainian Diaspora* (London: Routledge, 2002). On the OUN's legacy on Ukrainian memory, see David R. Marples, *Heroes and Villains: Creating National History in Contemporary Ukraine* (New York: Central European University Press, 2007).

2   [Redacted] Report on the assassination of Minister Pieracki, NARA, RG 263, E ZZ-18, B 80, Mykola Lebed Name File, v. 1.

3   On Lebed's post SSU Operational Memorandum No. MGH-391 on Operation Belladonna, December 27, 1946, NARA, RG 263, E ZZ-19, B 9, Aerodynamic: Operations, v. 9, f. 1. Lebed only privately admitted years later having trained at Zakopane in 1940. See RG 263, E ZZ-18, B 80, Mykola Lebed Name File, v. 3.

4   Frank Golczewski, "Shades of Grey: Reflections on Jewish-Ukrainian and German-Ukrainian Relations in Galicia," in *The Shoah in Ukraine: History, Testimony, Memorialization*, ed., Ray Brandon and Wendy Lower (Bloomington: Indiana University Press, 2008), pp. 133, 136.

5   See the Einsatzgruppe C order of November 1941 printed in *Ukraine During World War II: History and Its Aftermath*, ed. Yury Boshyk (Edmonton: Canadian Institute of Ukrainian Studies, 1986), p. 175.

6   See the "The Ukrainian Element," undated, NARA, RG 263, E ZZ-19, B 58, QRPLUMB, v. 1, n.1.

7   Quoted Tadeusz Piotrowski, *Genocide and Rescue in Wolyn: Recollections of the Ukrainian Nationalist Ethnic Cleansing Campaign against Poles During World War II* (Jefferson, NC: McFarland, 2000), p. 177.

8   Quoted in Karel C. Berkhoff and Marco Carynnyk, "The Organization of Ukrainian Nationalists and Its Attitude Toward Germans and Jews: Jaroslav Stes'ko's 1941 *Zhyttiepys*," *Harvard Ukrainian Studies*, v. 23, n. 3-4, p. 152.

9   Quoted Berkhoff and Carynnyk, "Organization," p. 154.

10 Quoted Berkhoff and Carynnyk, "Organization," p. 154.

11 Figure in Dieter Pohl, *Nationalsozialistische Judenverfolgung in Ostgalizien, 1941–1944: Organisation und Durchführung eines staatlichen Massenverbrechens* (Munich, 1997), p. 67.

12 Berkhoff and Carynnyk, "Organization," p. 154.

13 Yehuda Bauer, *The Death of the Shtetl* (New Haven: Yale University Press, 2010), p. 99.

14 Moshe Maltz, *Years of Horror-Glimpse of Hope: The Diary of a Family in Hiding* (New York: Shengold, 1993) [hereafter Maltz Diary], December 1943, p. 109.

15 Maltz Diary, November 1944, p. 147.

16 Quoted in Timothy Snyder, *The Reconstruction of Nations: Poland, Ukraine, Lithuania, Belarus 1569–1999* (New Haven: Yale University Press, 2003), p. 165.

17 Maltz Diary, November 1943, p. 107.

18 Timothy Snyder, "'To Resolve the Ukrainian Problem Once and For All': The Ethnic Cleansing of Ukrainians in Poland, 1943–1947"), *Journal of Cold War Studies*, v. 1, n. 2 (1999): 99.

19 Maltz Diary, November 1944, p. 147.

20 See the document excerpts printed in Piotrowsky, *Genocide and Rescue in Wolyn*, p. 211–13.

21 On the relationship between the UHVR, the OUN/B and the UPA in 1946, see the SSU Operational Memorandum No. MGH-391 on Operation Belladonna, December 27, 1946, NARA, RG 263, E ZZ-19, B 9, Aerodynamic: Operations, v. 9, f. 1.

22 SR/W2 to SR/WC, SR/DC, EE/SSS, January 13, 1952, NARA, RG 263, E ZZ-19, B 10, Aerodynamic: Operations, v. 10, f. 1. Also see Stetsko's accounts in NARA, RG 263, E ZZ-18, B 126, Name File Yaroslav Stetsko, v. 1, 2.

23 Satzewich, *Ukrainian Diaspora*, pp. 92, 96.

24 Rough data is in NARA, RG 319, IRR TS Banderist Activity, Czechoslovakia, v. 2.

25 For this and other interrogations see NARA, RG 263, E ZZ-19, B 11, Aerodynamic: Operations, v. 13.

26 Quoted Myroslav Yurkovich, "Ukrainian Nationalists and DP Politics," 1945–50, in *The Refugee Experience: Ukrainian Displaced Persons after World War II*, ed., Wsevolod W. Isajiz, et. al., (Edmonton, Canadian Institute of Ukrainian Studies Press, 1992), p. 135.

27 Special Agent Fred A. Stelling, Memorandum for the Officer in Charge, August 1, 1947, TS Organization of Banderist Movement, RG 319, IRR Bandera, Stephan, D 184850.

28 AC, MOB to Chief, FBM, MGM-A-1148, NARA, RG 263, E ZZ-18, B 57, Ivan Hrinioch Name File.

29 "Platform of the Ukrainian Supreme Liberation Council," July 15, 1944, NARA, RG 263, E ZZ-19, B 58, QRPLUMB, v. 1, n. 2.

30 "Summary – Joint OSO/OPC Report on the Ukrainian Resistance Movement, December 12, 1950, NARA, RG 263, E ZZ-19, B 9, Aerodynamic: Operations, v. 9, f. 1.

31 Chief of Station Karlsruhe to Chief, FBM, Project ICON, MGM-A-793, October 20, 1948, NARA, RG 263, E ZZ-19, B 9, Aerodynamic: Operations, v. 9, f. 1; SR/W2 to SR/WC, May 22, 1952, NARA, RG 263, E ZZ-19, Aerodynamic, v. 10, f. 2. Background of ZPUHVR-ZChOUN Relations, undated, NARA, RG 263, E ZZ-19, B 10, Aerodynamic: Operations, v. 10, f. 2. See also the summary of the break in "The Ukrainian Element," undated, NARA, RG 263, E ZZ-19, B 58, QRPLUMB, v. 1, n. 1.

32 EEIs for Interrogation of UPA Refugees, September 11, 1945, NARA, RG 319, IRR TS Banderist Activity CSR, v. 1, D 190425.

33 See partial reports designated as follows: Preliminary Reports I and Informant Report 35520 [undated], NARA, RG 319, IRR TS Banderist Activity CSR, v. 1, D 190425. See also Special Agent M.L Boraczek to Commanding Officer, 970th CIC Detachment, Region V, September 29, 1947, NARA, RG 319, IRR TS Banderist Activity, Czechoslovakia, v. 2, D 190425. See also Special Agent William E. Larned, VI-4464.1, September 14, 1947, NARA, RG 319, IRR TS Banderist Activity CSR, v. 1, D 190425.

34 Special Agent William E. Larned, VI-4464.1, September 14, 1947, NARA, RG 319, IRR TS Banderist Activity CSR, v. 1, D 190425.

35 Special Agent Eugene J. Memorandum for the Officer in Charge, UPA Activities, Interrogation of Four UPA Officers, September 14, 1947, NARA, RG 319, IRR TS Banderist Activity CSR, v. 1, D 190425.

36 Special Agent Fred A. Stelling, Memorandum for the Officer in Charge, August 1, 1947, NARA, RG 319, IRR TS Organization of Banderist Movement, D 184850; Special Agent Eugene J. Memorandum for the Officer in Charge, UPA Activities, Interrogation of Four UPA Officers, September 14, 1947, NARA, RG 319, IRR TS Banderist Activity CSR, v. 1, D 190425.

37 Undated Ukrainian statements, NARA, RG 319, IRR TS Banderist Activity Czechoslovakia, v. 2, D 190425.

38 Lt. Col. John L. Inskeep to Commanding Officer, 430th CIC Detachment, September 26, 1947, NARA, RG 319, IRR TS Banderist Activity CSR, v. 1, D 190425, v. 1; Special Agent Eugene J. Memorandum for the Officer in Charge, UPA Activities, Interrogation of Four UPA Officers, September 14, 1947, NARA, RG 319, IRR TS Banderist Activity CSR, v. 1, D 190425, v. 1; Special Agent William E. Larned, VI-4506.2, September 22, 1947, NARA, RG 319, IRR TS Banderist Activity CSR, v. 1, D 190425; Special Agent Fred A. Stelling, Memorandum for the Officer in Charge, August 1, 1947, RG 319, IRR TS Organization of Banderist Movement, D 184850.

39 Special Agent Daniel Osadchuk, Memorandum for the Officer in Charge, IV-2633, October 31, 1947, RG 319, IRR TS Banderist Activity Czechoslovakia, v. 2, D 190425.

40 Memorandum for the Officer in Charge, UPA Activities, Interrogation of Four UPA Officers, September 14, 1947, NARA, RG 319, IRR TS Banderist Activity CSR, v. 1, D 190425, v. 1.

41 Brand telegram, November 25, 1947, NARA, RG 319, IRR TS Banderist Activity Czecholovakia, v. 2, D 190425.

42 Bantsyrev to Brig. Gen T. L. Harrold, Director Civil Affairs, HQ EUCOM, No. 143, November 22, 1947, NARA, RG 319, IRR TS Banderist Activity Czechoslovakia, v. 2, D 190425.

43 Counterintelligence Report No. Z-70, September 16, 1947, NARA, RG 319, IRR TS Banderist Activity CSR, v. 1, D 190425.

44 Burds, *The Early Cold War in Soviet West Ukraine*, p. 12. This report does not follow Burds's conclusion that CIC hid Bandera from the Soviets.

45 AB-51, Amzon to AB-43, Munich, FSRO-656, October 28, 1946, NARA, RG 263, E ZZ-18, Stephen Bandera Name File, v. 1.

46 Bandera, Stephan A., June 4, 1948, NARA, RG 263, E ZZ-18, B 6, Stephen Bandera Name File, v. 1; XII Bandera, Stefan Andrejevich, Memo of July 1947, NARA, RG 319, IRR Bandera Movement, v. E, D 137656.

47 Special Agent Vadja V. Kolombatovic, III-M-943, May 6, 1947, NARA, RG 319, IRR Bandera Movement, v. E, D 137656.

48 Maj. Earl S. Browning, to Commanding Officer, CIC Region I, May 1, 1947, NARA, RG 319, IRR Bandera Movement, v. E, D 137656,

49 On early contacts with the UHVR, see Operational Memorandum, Operation Belladonna, No. MGH-391, December 27, 1946, NARA, RG 263, E ZZ-19, B 9, Aerodynamic: Operations, v. 9, f 1.

50 Chief of Station Karlsruhe to Chief FBM, MGM-A-793, October 28, 1948, NARA, RG 263, E ZZ-19, B 9, Aerodynamic: Operations, v. 9, f. 2.

51 SR/W2 to SR/WC, SR/DC, EE/SSS, January 13, 1952, NARA, RG 663, E ZZ-19, B 10, Aerodynamic: Operations, v. 10, f. 1.

52 CIA/State Department-SIS/Foreign Office Talks On Operations Against the USSR, April 23, 1951, NARA, RG 263, E ZZ-19, B 9, Aerodynamic: Operations, v. 9, f. 2.

53 See the report of November 1944 printed in Piotrowsky, *Genocide and Rescue in Wolyn*, p. 213.

54 This information comes from the notebook of Hermann Baun, a former Abwehr officer whose wartime operations were aimed at the USSR. After the war he became a section chief in the Gehlen Organization but fell out of favor. He was continually interested using ethnic groups in the Soviet Union to weaken it. See MGLA-11061, March 27, 1952, NARA, RG 263, E ZZ-18, B 126, Jaroslav Stetsko Name File, v. 1.

55 CIA/State Department – SIS/Foreign Office Talks of Operations Against the USSR, Exchange of Operational Data, Restricted Annex to Minutes of Session IV, April 24, 1951, NARA, RG 263, E ZZ-19, B 9, Aerodynamic: Operations, v. 9, f. 2.

56 CIA/State Department – SIS/Foreign Office Talks On Operations Against the USSR, April 23, 1951, NARA, RG 263, E ZZ-19, B 9, Aerodynamic: Operations, v. 9, f. 2.

57 Ukrainian Resistance: SIS Comment on CIA Intelligence Appreciation, April 1951, NARA, RG 263, E ZZ-19, B 9, Aerodynamic: Operations, v. 9, f. 2.

58 CIA/State Department – SIS/Foreign Office Talks On Operations Against the USSR, April 23, 1951, NARA, RG 263, E ZZ-19, B 9, Aerodynamic: Operations, v. 9, f. 2.

59 CIA/State Department – SIS/Foreign Office Talks On Operations Against the USSR, April 23, 1951, NARA, RG 263, E ZZ-19, B 9, Aerodynamic: Operations, v. 9, f. 2.

60 CIA/State Department – SIS/Foreign Office Talks On Operations Against the USSR, April 23, 1951, NARA, RG 263, E ZZ-19, B 9, Aerodynamic: Operations, v. 9, f. 2.

61 CIA/State Department–SIS/Foreign Office Talks On Operations Against the USSR, April 23, 1951, NARA, RG 263, E ZZ-19, B 9, Aerodynamic: Operations, v. 9, f. 2.

62 "Our Relations with the Ukrainian Nationalists and the Crisis over Bandera," Attached to EGQA-37253, March 12, 1954, NARA, RG 263, E ZZ-19, B 10, Aerodynamic: Operations, v. 10, f. 2.

63 "Our Relations with the Ukrainian Nationalists and the Crisis over Bandera," Attached to EGQA-37253, March 12, 1954, NARA, RG 263, E ZZ-19, B 10, Aerodynamic: Operations, v. 10, f. 2.

64 Quoted in "Our Relations with the Ukrainian Nationalists and the Crisis over Bandera," Attached to EGQA-37253, March 12, 1954, NARA, RG 263, E ZZ-19, B 10, Aerodynamic: Operations, v. 10, f. 2.

65 "Our Relations with the Ukrainian Nationalists and the Crisis over Bandera," Attached to EGQA-37253, March 12, 1954, NARA, RG 263, E ZZ-19, B 10, Aerodynamic: Operations, v. 10, f. 2. For the entire effort at reconciliation, see the contents of this entire folder. On Bishop Ivan Buczko's threats to excommunicate Hrinioch, see SR/3 W-2 to Chief, SR/3, July 27, 1954, NARA, RG 263, E ZZ-19, B 10, Aerodynamic: Operations, v. 11, f. 1.

66 SR/3 W-2 to Chief, SR/3, July 27, 1954, NARA, RG 263, E ZZ-19, B 10, Aerodynamic: Operations, v. 11, f. 1.

67 See the assessment in Dorril, *MI6*, pp. 244–45.

68 [Redacted] to Director of Security, January 9, 1956, NARA, RG 263, E ZZ-18, B 6, Stephen Bandera Name File, v. 1; Chief of Base Munich to Chief, SR, EGMA-19914, March 29, 1956, NARA, RG 263, E ZZ-18, B 6, Stephen Bandera Name File, v. 2 and enclosures; Deputy Director, Plans, to Department of State, July 1, 1957, NARA, RG 263, E ZZ-18, B 126, Jaroslav Stetsko Name File, v. 1; Joint US-UK Conference, January 20, 1955, NARA, RG 263, E ZZ-19, B 10, Aerodynamic: Operations, v. 12, n. 1; Director, CIA to [Redacted], DIR 00782, March 2, 1956, NARA, RG 263, E ZZ-19, B 11, Aerodynamic: Operations, v. 13.

69 Joint US-UK Conference, January 20, 1955, NARA, RG 263, E ZZ-19, B 10, Aerodynamic: Operations, v. 12, f. 1.

70 Director, CIA to [Redacted], DIR 00782, March 2, 1956, NARA, RG 263, E ZZ-19, B 11, Aerodynamic: Operations, v. 13.

71 Pullach to Director, Pull 3810, March 29, 1956, NARA, RG 263, E ZZ-19, B 11, Aerodynamic: Operations, v. 13.

72 Director, CIA to Pullach, Dir 05678, April 2, 1956, NARA, RG 263, E ZZ-19, B 11, Aerodynamic: Operations, v. 13.

73 Munich to Director, MUCO 033, September 5, 1956, NARA, RG 263, E ZZ-19, B 11, Aerodynamic: Operations, v. 14, f. 1.

74 Munich to Director, MUNI 5527, July 23, 1959, NARA, RG 263, E ZZ-19, B 12, Aerodynamic: Operations, v. 17.

75 The CIA cryptonym used in the records for Herre was HERDAHL. See Munich to Director, September 24, 1959, NARA, RG 263, E ZZ-18, B 6, Stephen Bandera Name File, v. 2.

76 Memorandum by Herre, Attachment to EGMA-45003, August 27, 1959, NARA, RG 263, E ZZ-18, B 6, Stephen Bandera Name File, v. 2.

77 Munich to Director, MUNI 5527, July 23, 1959, NARA, RG 263, E ZZ-19, B 12, Aerodynamic: Operations, v. 17.

78 Memorandum for Chief, SR/3, September 4, 1959, NARA, RG 263, E ZZ-19, B 12, Aerodynamic: Operations, v. 17.

79 Chief of Base, Munich to Chief, SR, EGMA-45003, October 5, 1959, NARA, RG 263, E ZZ-18, B 6, Stephen Bandera Name File, v. 2.

80 The full West German investigative story is in Memorandum for the Record, April 22, 1976, NARA, RG 263, E ZZ-18, B 6, Stephen Bandera Name File, v. 2.

81 Page to Department of State, October 26, 1959, NARA, RG 263, E ZZ-18, B 6, Stephen Bandera Name File, v. 2.

82 See especially NARA, RG 263, E ZZ-19, B 20, Aerodynamic: Operations, v. 36, f. 1.

83 [Redacted], Meeting with UPHILL [BND] Representative, May 26, 1961, NARA, RG 263, E ZZ-19, B 14, Aerodynamic: Operations, v. 21, f. 2.

84 [Redacted] to Chief, FDM, Cartel 2 Debriefing Report, December 16, 1949, NARA, RG 263, E ZZ-19, B 9, Aerodynamic: Operations, v. 9, f. 1.

85 SSU Operational Memorandum No. MGH-391 on Operation Belladonna, December 27, 1946, NARA, RG 263, E ZZ-19, B 9, Aerodynamic: Operations, v. 9, f. 1.

86 Joint OSO-OPC Report on Ukrainian Resistance Movement, December 12, 1950, NARA, RG 263, E ZZ-19, B 9, Aerodynamic: Operations, v. 9, f. 1.

87 Card Ref. D 82270, July 22, 1947, NARA, RG 319, E 134B, B 757, Mykola Lebed IRR Personal File, Box 757.

88 Special Agent Camille S. Hajdu, Memorandum for the Officer in Charge, November 17, 1947, NARA, RG 319, E134B, Box 757, Mykola Lebed IRR Personal File.

89 Norman J.W. Goda, "Nazi Collaborators in the United States: What the FBI Knew," in Richard Breitman, et. al., *U.S. Intelligence and the Nazis* (New York: Cambridge, 2005), pp. 251–52.

90 Chief of Station Karlsruhe to Chief, FBM, Project ICON, MGM-A-793, October 20, 1948, NARA, RG 263, E ZZ-19, B 9, Aerodynamic: Operations, v. 9, f. 1; Attachment to EGOW-1653, June 30, 1960, NARA, RG 263, E ZZ-19, B 13, Aerodynamic: Operations, v. 19, f. 1. The Hrinioch-Lebed group by this time was also insolvent and needed the help. Hrinioch was convinced that the Ukraine could only become independent with U.S. aid. See AC, MOB to Chief, FBM, MGM-A-1148, NARA, RG 263, E ZZ-18, B 57, Ivan Hrinioch Name File.

91 [Redacted] to Chief, FDM, Cartel 2 Debriefing Report, December 16, 1949, NARA, RG 263, E ZZ-19, B 9, Aerodynamic: Operations, v. 9, f. 1.

92 CIA Assistant Director Allen Dulles's personal intervention in his case with the Immigration and Naturalization Service, which saw in Lebed "a clear-cut deportation case" owing to his wartime activities. See Goda, "Nazi Collaborators in the United States," pp. 251–55. The second release of the CIA File on Lebed has the relevant documentation on Dulles's role. See NARA, RG 263, E ZZ-18, Box 80, Mykola Lebed Name File, v. 1.

93 [Redacted] to Chief, FDM, Cartel 2 Debriefing Report, December 16, 1949, NARA, RG 263, E ZZ-19, B 9, Aerodynamic: Operations, v. 9, f. 1.Memorandum for the Record, February 15, 1950, NARA, RG 263, E ZZ-19, B 9, Aerodynamic Operations, v. 9, f. 1.

94 SR/W2 to SR/WC, May 21, 1952, NARA, RG 263, E ZZ 19, B 10, Aerodynamic: Operations, v. 10, f. 2.

95 Special Agent Daniel Barna, Memorandum for the Officer in Charge, April 19, 1949, NARA, RG 319, E 134B, Box 757, Mykola Lebed IRR Personal File.

96 Goda, "Nazi Collaborators in the United States," p. 253.

97 Joint OSO-OPC Report On the Ukrainian Resistance Movement, December 12, 1950, NARA, RG 263, E ZZ-19, B 9, Aerodynamic: Operations, v. 9, f. 1.

98 Operations into Ukraine, November 28, 1950, NARA, RG 263, E ZZ-19, B 9, Aerodynamic: Operations, v. 9, f. 1. Wisner to Director of Central Intelligence, Joint OSO/OPC Report on the Ukrainian Resistance Movement," January 4, 1951, and attachments, NARA, RG 263, E ZZ-19, B 9, Aerodynamic: Operations, v. 9, f. 1.

99 Ukrainian Resistance, April 1953, NAA, RG 263, E ZZ-19, B 10, Aerodynamic: Operations, v. 11, f. 1; Questionnaire, June 30, 1957, NARA, RG 263, E ZZ-19, B 11, Aerodynamic: Operations, v. 15, f. 1.

100 Tentative Plan of Cover for Ukrainian Study Group, December 2, 1953, NARA, RG 263, E ZZ-19, B 10, Aerodynamic: Operations, v. 11, f. 1; Attachment B to EGMA-[redacted], Operational Matters and Comments, undated, NARA, RG 263, E ZZ-19, B 11, Aerodynamic: Operations, v. 14, f. 2; Chief, Soviet Bloc Division, Memorandum for Assistant Deputy Director of Plans, June 12, 1968, NARA, RG 263, E ZZ-19, B 9, Aerodynamic: Development and Plans, v. 5.

101 Aerodynamic Renewal, FY 1970, NARA, RG 263, E ZZ-19, B 9, Aerodynamic: Development and Plans, v. 7; IG Survey Group on Proprietaries, December 8, 1966, NARA, RG 263, E ZZ-19, B 19, Aerodynamic: Operations, v. 35, f. 1. Memorandum for the 303 Committee, October 30, 1967, NARA, RG 263, E ZZ-19, B 20, Aerodynamic: Operations, v. 37. f. 1.

102 On the exact relationship between ZH UHVR, Prolog, and Aerodynamic, see Memorandum for IG Survey Group on Proprietaries, December 8, 1966, NARA, RG 263, E ZZ-19, B 19, Aerodynamic: Operations, v. 35, f. 1.

103 Questionnaire, June 30, 1957, NARA, RG 263, E ZZ-19, B 11, Aerodymnamic: Operations, v. 15, f. 1; Project Aerodynamic, Renewal FY 1959, September 28, 1958, NARA, RG 263, E ZZ-19, Aerodynamic, v. 3.

104 Project Aerodynamic, Renewal FY 1959, September 28, 1958, NARA, RG 263, E ZZ-19, B 8, Aerodynamic: Development and Plans, v. 3.

105 Project Aerodynamic, Renewal FY 1959, September 28, 1958, NARA, RG 263, E ZZ-19, B 19, Aerodynamic: Operations, v. 34; Project Aerodynamic, Renewal FY 1961, October 7, 1960, NARA, RG 263, E ZZ-19, B 19, Aerodynamic: Operations, v. 34; Memorandum for Chief, SR/3, August 16, 1961, NARA, RG 263, E ZZ-19, B 19, Aerodynamic: Operations, v. 34; David Murphy, Chief, SR Division, to Deputy Director for Plans, April 15, 1966, NARA, RG 263, E ZZ-19, B 19, Aerodynamic: Operations, v. 35; Project Aerodynamic Renewal, FY 67, NARA, RG 263, E ZZ-19, B 19, Aerodynamic:

Operations, v. 35; Aerodynamic Project Renewal, FY 70, NARA, RG 263, E ZZ-19, B 9, Aerodynamic: Development and Plans, v. 7; Memorandum for the 303 Committee, October 30, 1967, NARA, RG 263, E ZZ-19, B 20, Aerodynamic: Operations, v. 37, f. 1. On spotting operations see NARA, RG 263, E ZZ-19, B 15-15, Aerodynamic: Operations, v. 21–24, and especially IG Survey Response Group on Proprietaries, December 8, 1966, RG 263, E ZZ-19, B 19, Aerodynamic: Operations, v. 35, f. 1 for Kaminsky's identity. Kaminsky was also a Ukrainian émigré writer.

106 Zvi Y. Gittelman, *A Century of Ambivalence: The Jews of Russia and the Soviet Union, 1881 to the Present* (Bloomington, IN: Indiana University Press, 2001) pp. 165–66.

107 Declaration of the Foreign Representation," April 6, 1964, NARA, RG 263, E ZZ-19, B 16, Aerodynamic, v. 28, f. 1.

108 See NARA, RG 263, E ZZ-19, B 16-17, Aerodynamic: Operations, v. 28–31.

109 Brzezinski to Director of Central Intelligence, March 20, 1979, NARA, RG 263, E ZZ-19, B 59, QRPLUMB, v. 3.

110 FY 1982 Renewal of Activity PDDYNAMIC, NARA, RG 263, E ZZ-19, B 59, QRPLUMB, v. 4.

111 NARA, RG 263, E ZZ-19, B 5, QRPLUMB, v. 5, f. 2.

CONCLUSION

This report discusses only a sample of newly released records, hinting at their overall richness. The 1.3 million Army files include thousands of titles of many more issues regarding wartime criminals, their pursuit, their arrest, their escape, and occasionally, their use by Allied and Soviet intelligence agencies. These include files on German war criminals, but also collaborators from the Baltic States, Belarus, Ukraine, Romania, Hungary, Croatia, and elsewhere. These files also include information on Allied and non-aligned states that had an interest in Axis personalities, including Great Britain, France, Italy, Argentina, and Israel.

The 1,110 re-released or newly released CIA name files are in most cases far more detailed than the files of the initial CIA release in 2001 and after. They contain a trove of information on Nazis who eventually worked for the Gehlen Organization or as Soviet spies after the war. They hold information about important Nazi officials who escaped and became figures of security interest in other countries spanning the globe from the Middle East to South America. Together, the Army and CIA records will keep scholars of World War II and the Cold War busy for many years.

The new files also have postwar intelligence on other subjects. The CIC kept close watch on other suspect groups, such as German communists, and kept thousands of files on them. They kept watch on politically active Jewish refugees in displaced persons camps. Indeed, there are many hundreds of newly released files concerning the remnant of European Jews who searched for a new life in Palestine or the United States. Thus the new records are of great interest to those researching a very broad range of topics from international Communism to the Jewish diaspora to the history of mass migration.

The declassification of intelligence-related material is a controversial subject, involving as it does the release of records formerly of national security interest. The current releases show, however, that the passage of years lessens the information's sensitivity while providing researchers access to raw information that is simply not available elsewhere. By their very nature, intelligence agencies attain and record information that other government or non-government organizations cannot. None of the chapters in this report could have been written without declassified intelligence records, nor could the many articles and books that will emerge as a result of the current release. The funding for declassification and the assurance that intelligence records are opened to the public thus preserve key aspects of world history. In the interest of understanding our past Congress should, in our view, ensure that such openness continues.

ACRONYMS

BfV	Bundesamt fur Verfassungsschutz (West Germany's domestic intelligence agency) Office for the Protection of the Constitution
BND	German Secret Service
CIC	U.S. Army Counterintelligence Corps
KPD	German Communist Party
KPÖ	Kommunistische Partei Osterreichs
IRR	Investigative Records Repository
NSDAP	Nationalsozialistische Deutsche Arbeiterpartei (Nazi Party)
OPC	Office of Policy Coordination
OSO	Office of Special Operations
OUN	Organization of Ukrainian Nationalists
ÖVP	Osterreichische Volkspartei
RSHA	Reichssicherheitshauptamt (Reich Security Main Office)
SD	Sicherheitsdienst (SS Intelligence Organization)
SDECE	Documentation and External Counterespionage Service (French Intelligence)
SIFAR	Italian Military Intelligence
SPÖ	Sozialdemokratische Partei Osterreichs
SRP	Socialist Reich Party
SSU	Strategic Services Unit
UHVR	Supreme Ukrainian Liberation Council
UPA	Ukrainian Insurgent Army
VdU	Verband der Unabhänginge
VVN	Union of Nazi Persecutees
WJC	World Jewish Congress

www.ingramcontent.com/pod-product-compliance
Lightning Source LLC
Chambersburg PA
CBHW081235090426
42738CB00016B/3313